INSIGHT ⊙ GUIDES

EXPLORE

QUÉBEC

PLAN & BOOK
YOUR TAILOR-MADE TRIP

 BRAZIL  CHILE  ECUADOR

TAILOR-MADE TRIPS & UNIQUE EXPERIENCES CREATED BY LOCAL TRAVEL EXPERTS AT INSIGHTGUIDES.COM/HOLIDAYS

Insight Guides has been inspiring travellers with high-quality travel content for over 45 years. As well as our popular guidebooks, we now offer the opportunity to book tailor-made private trips completely personalised to your needs and interests.
By connecting with one of our local experts, you will directly benefit from their expertise and local know-how, helping you create memories that will last a lifetime.

HOW INSIGHTGUIDES.COM/HOLIDAYS WORKS

STEP 1

Pick your dream destination and submit an enquiry, or modify an existing itinerary if you prefer.

STEP 2

Fill in a short form, sharing details of your travel plans and preferences with a local expert.

STEP 3

Your local expert will create your personalised itinerary, which you can amend until you are completely satisfied.

STEP 4

Book securely online. Pack your bags and enjoy your holiday! Your local expert will be available to answer questions during your trip.

CONTENTS

COVID-19 Updates

While travelling in Canada, be sure to heed all local laws, travel advice and hygiene measures. While we've done all we can to make sure this guide is accurate and up to date, be sure to check ahead.

ART LOVERS

Artistic highlights include the Musée d'Art Contemporain de Montréal (route 2) in Montréal. Musée des Beaux Arts de Sherbrooke (route 5) and the Centre d'art Diane-Dufresne (route 6) also hold collections of fine art.

RECOMMENDED ROUTES FOR...

CHILDREN

Go kayaking, hiking or beluga whale spotting along the Fjord du Saguenay (route 10). Head to the Vieux-Port of Montréal for the big wheel and the Centre des Sciences de Montréal (route 1).

ESCAPING THE CROWDS

There are quite a few places covered in this book that can make you feel like you're a long way from anywhere. To escape the crowds, you can only need to visit the isolated towns of Natashquan and Kegashka (route 11).

FOODIES

Montréal's restaurants are world-renowned (routes 1 and 2), while many of the vineyards of the Route des Vins (route 4) also knock out excellent food. Foodies should also spend time on the Île d'Orléans (route 8).

HISTORY BUFFS

Québec City (route 7) was where New France got its start in 1608, and remains crammed with fine historic remnants. Trois-Rivières (route 6) was established next and remains a fascinating city to explore.

ISLAND FUN

There's lots of island fun to be had on this route. For starters, you can take a trip to the Île d'Orléans (route 8). The islands of the Mingan Archipelago (route 11) are stunning, as are the trails on l'Île-Bonaventure (route 13).

MANORS AND GARDENS

The Domaine Joly-de Lotbinière features some of the most beautiful gardens in Canada (route 6). Île d'Orléans (route 9) also has some well-preserved manor houses, plus La Seigneurie, a lavender farm with beautiful gardens.

NATURE LOVERS

Go whale-watching off Tadoussac (route 10) or Rivière-du-Loup (route 12), hike through Parc National Forillon (route 13) and Parc National du Mont-Tremblant (route 3), or kayak the waterways of Parc national des Hautes-Gorges-de-la-Rivière-Malbaie (route 9).

INTRODUCTION

An introduction to Québec's geography, customs and culture, plus illuminating background information on cuisine, history and what to do when you're there.

EXPLORE QUÉBEC

Snow-capped peaks, mesmerizing fjords and some of the finest food in the world. Québec is crammed with natural wonders, but also has its own rich cultural identity, blending French traditions with kayaking, lobster fishing and maple sugar shacks.

Canada's largest province, Québec stretches from the temperate farmland in the south to the Arctic tundra in the north, covering over 1.3 million square kilometres. Beyond the major hubs of Montréal and Québec City nature rules supreme, with the relatively mild climate along the St Lawrence supporting a patchwork of farms and small towns, giving way to great swathes of wilderness in the interior – moose, caribou, wolverine and bears fill the forests and in many places humans have barely made inroads. From the language to the cuisine, Québec is distinct from the rest of the continent.

Québec is the only French-speaking society in North America. After the colony was transferred to British rule, the Québécois were allowed to maintain their language and Catholic religion, which ensured large families and a prevalence of French-speakers – a political move termed the *revanche du berceau* ("revenge of the cradle"). Centuries later, the result is a unique blend of North American and European influence and a province with a fascinating dual personality.

GEOGRAPHY AND LAYOUT

The area covered in this book is vast, much of it isolated wilderness hemmed in between Hudson's Bay, the St Lawrence River and Canada's eastern Atlantic coast. In reality, the majority of the population of Québec lives on or close to the St. Lawrence. The tours in this book begin with Montréal, the biggest city in Québec, then proceed geographically across the province from west to east.

COVID-19 Updates

In early 2020, COVID-19 swept across the globe, being categorized as a pandemic by the World Health Organization in March. While travelling in Canada, be sure to heed all local laws, travel advice and hygiene measures; flouting these means risking your own health but can also put a strain on local communities and their medical infrastructure. While we've done all we can to make sure this guide is accurate and up to date, permanent closures and changed opening hours are likely in the wake of coronavirus, so be sure to check ahead.

The Old Montréal

The focus then shifts to Québec City, with routes that lead northeast along both sides of the St Lawrence – most routes link to each other, making longer trips possible. You'll need a car to make the most out of the area, as public transport is limited to a handful of long-distance bus lines and railway routes. Most cities are small enough to explore on foot, though taxis are usually easy to find.

HISTORY

Various Indigenous groups and communities have lived in the province for millennia. The French were the first Europeans to explore the area, beginning with Jacques Cartier in 1535; Samuel de Champlain founded Québec City in 1608 and Montréal was established in 1642 at the centre of "New France". Decades of French-British rivalry in North America culminated in the French and Indian War (1754–1763).

The turning point took place in 1759 with the Battle of the Plains of Abraham, a British victory that resulted in the capture of Québec City. The 1840 Act of Union joining Lower and Upper Canada can be seen as a deliberate attempt to

---

DON'T LEAVE QUÉBEC WITHOUT...

Wandering the streets of Vieux-Montréal. Old Montréal's cobblestone streets are lined with lively bars and centuries-old buildings and monuments. See page 26

Sampling poutine and Québécois cuisine. The province's beloved comfort food comes in numerous styles, while Québécois cuisine is innovative and always tasty. See page 14

Visiting the Musée des Beaux-Arts. Explore Canada's oldest museum, which showcases the country's most impressive collection of Canadian art. See page 35

Sipping your way around La Route des Vins. Sample the white, red, ice and fruit wines of Québec's Cantons de l'Est. See page 44

Exploring Vieux-Québec. The only walled city in North America is full of museums, cobbled streets, historic churches and romantic nooks and crannies. See page 61

Hiking in Parc National Forillon. At the very tip of the Gaspé Peninsula, this exquisite national park has it all: spectacular setting, iconic wildlife and a restored fishing village. See page 97

Cruising Saguenay Fjord. See the densely wooded slopes and cliffs of this vast fjord by boat, or take a whale-watching cruise from Tadoussac. See page 81

Cycling La Route Verte. Take in some of Québec's most scenic countryside while cycling this thoroughly enjoyable network of bike trails, from Lac Saint-Jean to the Cantons de l'Est.

Kayaking the Mingan Archipelago. Kayak around the eerie "flowerpot" islands dotted by immense wind-sculpted rock formations and teeming with wildlife.

Autumn in Hautes-Gorges-de-la-Riviere-Malbaie National Park

marginalize francophone opinion within an English-speaking state.

The shake-up of Québec society finally came about with the so-called Quiet Revolution in the 1960s. The provincial government took control of welfare, health and education from the church. Since 2018, the province has been led by François Legault's centre-right Coalition Avenir Québec, which has ruled out another referendum, though it does support increased autonomy.

CLIMATE

Because of its size, the climate of Québec varies wildly, from Arctic to relatively mild "humid continental". In reality, tourists rarely frequent the colder, northern areas, and the region along the St Lawrence River experiences warm, humid summers and long, cold winters, though even here temperatures can drop or rise as much as 17°C (30 °F) in less than a day. Montréal experiences average temperatures of -6°C to -15°C in January, and 16°C to 26°C in July; Québec City is only slightly cooler, but in Sept-Îles, temperatures range -10°C to -21°C in January, and 11°C to 20°C in July. Rain tends to peak July to September, but snow blankets the region through much of the winter.

POPULATION

The population of Québec is a little over 8.5 million – beyond Montréal and Québec City population density is very low and towns are relatively small. Some 30 percent of the population claim French origin. Montréal is a multicultural city, with substantial Haitian, Arab, Latin American, Chinese and South Asian communities, as well as a large Jewish population.

Indigenous Québec

This travel guide describes places that include the traditional lands and Treaty territories of many Indigenous Peoples, including the Huron-Wendat, Innu, and Mohawk. Travelling offers us the privilege of being a guest among our hosts and building relationships with them. As you travel, take the opportunity to learn the history of a place; support Indigenous businesses and artists; and make connections with the people who continue to inhabit these lands.

LOCAL CUSTOMS

As "French Canada", Québec does differ from the cultural traditions of much of the rest of the country, though it's not quite as different as advertised, and it's not quite France either. French speakers will usually pick up the quite distinctive Québécois accent, which is quite different to the French spoken in Paris (and most of France) and the

Celebrating Fete nationale du Québec

Acadian French accent; it's a bit like comparing US and British English. In general, French cultural traditions are more pronounced in rural areas such as the Gaspé.

POLITICS AND ECONOMICS

Since 2018 the premier of Québec has been François Legault, whose Coalition Avenir Québec (CAQ) won the provincial election in a landslide. Dominique Anglade now leads the Liberals – the first woman to have the job. The next election is scheduled to take place by October 2022, though it seems unlikely any party will unseat the CAQ.

Québec's economy is stronger than ever before (at least before the COVID pandemic), with the second largest provincial GDP in Canada after Ontario. Though the services sector remains most important, the province also benefits from abundant natural resources. Aerospace is a major sector; the Port of Montréal is the second biggest container port in Canada; and Hydro-Quebec is Canada's leader in hydroelectric energy production. Mining and the pulp and paper industries remain important.

TOP TIPS FOR VISITING QUÉBEC

Make reservations. It's crucial to book your accommodation well ahead of your stay (especially in the far north), as well as whale-watching trips in summer.

Bears. Hikers especially should be aware that black bears are present throughout Québec, though attacks are very rare. If a black bear approaches you, speak calmly and firmly, avoid eye contact, and back away slowly. Never run or try to climb a tree. Do not "play dead". Polar bears are also present in the far north of Québec, but you are extremely unlikely to get anywhere near them.

Tourism websites. Québec has an excellent tourism department with an extremely useful website: www.bonjourquebec.com.

Provincial holidays. In terms of provincial holidays, schools and most businesses are closed on these days in Québec, in addition of Canadian national holidays (Québec celebrates Victoria Day as "National Patriots' Day"): Either Good Friday or Easter Monday (though many employers allow both days). June 24: Fête nationale du Québec (Saint-Jean-Baptiste Day). "Construction Holiday" (Vacances de la construction): official holiday period of the construction industry over last two weeks of July – many other Québécois take vacations at the same time.

Time zones. Most of Québec follows Eastern Standard Time (GMT-5), and observes Daylight Savings Times. There are a couple of exceptions. The Magdalen Islands follow Atlantic Standard Time (GMT−4), with Daylight Savings; while the far east of Québec, beyond the Natashquan River, follows AST but does not use to daylight time (only Kegashka falls in this area in this book).

Montréal café

FOOD AND DRINK

Québec cuisine is a remarkable combination of French and Canadian; bistros, cafés, baguettes and croissants blended with fresh lobster, moose and mussels to create something wholly unique. Small-batch producers and craft breweries flourish here.

Québec's culinary scene has been influenced in more recent years by Italian, Greek, Middle Eastern and Asian flavours, with Montréal one of the world's great foodie cities. But even the province's smaller communities often boast surprisingly good restaurants, supplied by a healthy roster of local farmers' markets, artisanal food producers (especially cheese and bread), wineries and beer-makers. At the top-end, the province has its own crop of celebrity chefs: the likes of Martin Picard, owner of *Au Pied de Cochon* (a favourite of the late Anthony Bourdain), *Joe Beef* co-owners/chefs David McMillan and Frédéric Morin, award-winning Anne Desjardins and Chuck Hughes, owner of *Garde Manger*.

QUÉBEC CUISINE

Québec is renowned for its outstanding French-style cuisine, blended with frontier, North American-style cooking and ingredients. Pork forms a major part of the local diet, both as a spicy pâté known as *creton*, and in *tourtière*, a minced pork pie. The oddly named *pâté chinois* ("Chinese pie") is another classic French Canadian dish, a bit like English shepherd's pie (made with beef), while *fèves au lard* is a hearty blend of red beans with bacon and maple syrup, doled out in big bowls.

There are also splendid thick pea and cabbage soups, beef pies (*cipâte*), and all sorts of ways to soak up maple syrup – *trempette* is bread drenched with it and topped with fresh cream. *Grands-pères* are round pastries infused with maple syrup, while *pouding chômeur* ("poor man's pudding") is a cake made by mixing the batter with hot syrup or caramel before baking.

Seafood is also incredibly popular: Arctic char, salmon and trout are the most popular local fish, while shellfish, lobster and crab are caught off the Gaspé Peninsula, Côte-Nord and the Magdalen Islands.

Classic French dishes such as *bœuf bourguignon*, *galettes* (buckwheat pancakes), meatball *ragout*, and chicken *vol-au-vent* are also widely popular. Quicker snacks include Québec's unofficial national dish, poutine – fries covered in melted mozzarella cheese or cheese curds and gravy – which is available at almost every restaurant throughout the province.

Montréal Style bagels

Maple syrup taffy candy

Montréal

A culinary destination that rivals the gourmet capitals of the world, Montréal is said to have the highest number of restaurants per capita in North America after New York City. It was *Toqué* – helmed by master chef Normand Laprise – that catapulted the city to the top culinary ranks, and since then numerous home-grown chefs have captured the world's attention. Montréal's ethnic diversity is amply displayed by the variety of cuisines available. The city has its own Chinatown just north of Vieux-Montréal, a Little Italy around Jean-Talon Métro (near the excellent Jean-Talon market) and a Greek community whose cheaper restaurants are concentrated along Prince Arthur. Most prominent of the international restaurants are the Eastern European establishments dotted around the city. Opened by Jewish immigrants, their speciality is smoked meat, served between huge chunks of rye bread with pickles on the side. Montréal comes a close second to New York as the bagel capital of the world; they're sold everywhere. The city has also long embraced the concept of *apportez votre vin* ("bring your own wine"), with a wide variety of lively "BYOW" restaurants.

Maple syrup and sugar shacks

Québec is by far the world's biggest producer of maple syrup, accounting for over 70 percent of global supply. Understandably, it plays a huge part in Québécois culture and cuisine. During the *"temps des sucres"* each March (during the peak maple sugar season), families flock to the province's famed sugar shacks,

---

Montréal-style Bagels

Smaller, thinner and denser than New York bagels, Montréal-style bagels have developed an equally fanatical following over the years. Introduced to the city in the early 20th century by Jewish immigrants, the two primary kinds – black-seed (poppy seed) and white-seed (sesame seed) – are traditionally baked in a wood-fired oven and accompanied with cream cheese "schmears". Locals still argue about which shop produces the best bagels, though the two oldest shops have the longest running rivalry. Fairmount Bagel (https://fairmountbagel.com) dates back to 1919, when it was opened as "Montreal Bagel Bakery", by Russian-émigré Isadore Shlafman. Legendary St-Viateur Bagel Shop (www.stviateurbagel.com) was opened in 1957 by Polish arrival and Buchenwald survivor Myer Lewkowicz – he learnt his trade at the old Montreal Bagel Bakery before striking out on his own. Other legendary Jewish delis nearby include smoked meat specialist Schwartz's (www.schwartzsdeli.com), which was established by Reuben Schwartz, a Jewish immigrant from Romania, in 1928. Wilensky's Light Lunch was founded in 1932 by Moe Wilensky, and is known for its grilled bologna sandwich – and for appearing the Mordecai Richler novel *The Apprenticeship of Duddy Kravitz*.

Jean–Talon farmers market

where they eat maple syrup poured on snow and other traditional dishes inevitably smothered with it. These days sugar shacks tend to open year-round (or during the main sugar making and maple harvest seasons, mid-Feb to early May and mid-Aug to end-Oct), serving up hearty, traditional meals in rustic surroundings. Martin Picard's Cabane à Sucre Au Pied de Cochon (https://aupieddecochon.ca), in St-Benoît de Mirabel (58km west of Montréal), is one of the more high-end examples.

WHERE TO EAT

You'll find a huge variety of restaurants in Montréal and Québec City serving international cuisines, but though the number of places to eat rapidly decreases beyond the cities, the variety and quality on offer is usually very high, even in the smallest communities. Local cafés and coffeeshops, bakeries and bistros abound, and every town has at least one gourmet restaurant in addition to the usual fast-food options.

Food and drink prices

Throughout this book, price guide for a two-course meal for one with an alcoholic drink:

$$$$ = over $75
$$$ = $51–75
$$ = $25–50
$ = below $25

Chain restaurants

All the usual fast-food suspects and chains are present in Québec. Local chains include Ben & Florentine (http://benandflorentine.com), the breakfast specialist founded in Saint-Laurent in 2008; Chez Ashton (https://chezashton.ca), best known for its poutine; Dunn's (www.dunnsfamous.com) Jewish-style diners; Sherbrooke's very own Eggsquis (https://eggsquis.com); all-day diner La Belle Province (http://restaurantlabelleprovince.com); Québécois fast food staple Lafleur (https://restolafleur.com); sub specialist Mike's (http://www.mikes.ca); Normandin pizza joints (https://restaurantnormandin.com); Smoke's Poutinerie (www.smokespoutinerie.com); and the rotisserie chicken at St-Hubert (www.st-hubert.com).

Food halls and markets

There are food halls and markets as well as fresh food stalls in the Québec, usually home to local vendors selling regional snacks and produce. Marché Bonsecours (see page 30) in Vieux-Montréal is one of the best examples but there are several others in the city, including Le Central (www.lecentral.ca), Time Out Market (www.timeoutmarket.com/montreal), and Le Cathcart (www.lecathcart.com). In Québec City there's the Grand Marché de Québec (www.legrandmarchedequebec.com), and the Marché public de Sainte-Foy. Local markets are worth seeking out across the province, with outdoor farmer's markets most prevalent May to October.

Organic radishes at a local farmer's market in Montréal

DRINKS

The legal drinking age is 18 in Québec, and unlike much of the rest of the country, beer and wine (not spirits) are sold at normal retail grocery stores.

Beer

Québec has been a prominent player in the huge explosion of craft or micro-brewed beers in North America since the 1980s, and today numerous small batch producers or *microbrasseries* compete with the Canadian and European mainstays. Brasserie Massawippi opened in 1982, becoming the first craft brewer in the province. In 1986, the Golden Lion Pub in Lennoxville (www.lionlennoxville.com) and Le Cheval Blanc (https://lechevalblanc.ca) in Montréal started serving their own craft beers. Since then microbreweries have popped up even in the smallest communities – highly-rated Microbrasserie Le Saint-Fût (http://lesaintfut.com) operates in tiny Saint-Fulgence. Other names to look out for are La Barberie in Québec City, Brasserie Dunham, À l'abri de la Tempête is the Magdalen Islands, Microbrasserie du Lac Saint-Jean, Le Trou du Diable in Shawinigan, Microbrasserie Dieu du Ciel! in Saint-Jérôme, and Microbrasserie La Memphré in Magog, among other 150 others.

Québec wine

Québécois love wine, and though the vintages made here can't quite compete with France, the quality is improving and every year; in 2018 the provincial government officially recognized the Protected Geographical Indication (PGI) "Quebec Wine" status. The most common grape varieties grown here are Maréchal Foch, Frontenac and De Chaunac (reds), and Vidal and Seyval blanc (whites). Ice wines, sparkling wines and fruit wines are also produced in Québec. Wine is produced in 146 vineyards divided into seven regions promoted by Wines of Québec (http://winesofquebec.com): Appalachian foothills and Appalachian Plateau in the Cantons-de-l'Est (see page 44); Deux-Montagnes; Lake Saint-Pierre; Monteregian Hills; Québec City and the banks of the St Lawrence; and Richelieu River Valley.

Officially recognized as a Protected Geographical Indication (PGI) in 2014, ice wine is produced at many Québec vineyards. It's made by pressing frozen grapes in cold outdoor air, allowing for production of a dense, sugary must with frozen water remaining trapped inside the pulp.

Ice cider

Ice cider is the cider equivalent of ice wine – made with frozen apples, which concentrates the sugars in the fruit, leading to a higher alcohol cider. Though ice wine originated in Europe and was initiated for the first time in Canada in the 1970s in British Columbia, ice cider is a genuine Québec invention. It was pioneered by Christian Barthomeuf in the Cantons de l'Est, who produced the first batch in 1989 (see page 44).

ENTERTAINMENT

Québec is home to a thriving arts and cultural scene, and with a rich legacy of live theatre, comedy and theatre, you can experience live shows most days of the week.

When it comes to nightlife in Québec, everything revolves around Montréal, and to a lesser extent Québec City. Beyond these two hubs, entertainment principally comprises local bars and microbreweries, community theatre and local folk bands, though major ski resorts like Mount Tremblant are known for their off-piste nightlife.

BARS AND CLUBS

Montréal has elevated joie de vivre to a high art – and nowhere more so than at the bars and clubs. The city's nightlife keeps going strong into the small hours of the morning, and you can expect bars to stay open until 3am. One of the liveliest after-dark areas is the bar-packed Plateau. Cutting a wide swath through the Plateau – and into the adjacent neighbourhood of Mile-End – is blvd St-Laurent, lined on both sides with an eclectic array of nightspots, from sleek lounges to dive bars.

Downtown, the action centres on rue Crescent, while Vieux-Montréal is increasingly buzzing with new hotel lounges, restaurant-bars and breezy terraces.

Québec City has far more relaxed nightlife than Montréal: an evening spent in an intimate bar or a jazz or blues soiree is more popular than a big gig or disco. Outside of the Festival d'Été in July, few major bands tour here, though there are plenty of spots to catch Québécois bands.

Québec City's main bar and nightclub strips are around rue St-Jean in Saint-Jean-Baptiste and rue St-Joseph in Saint-Roch; both have lively bars and LGBTQ nightspots oozing atmosphere.

LIVE MUSIC

Montréal has been a live music hub for decades. Some of the most atmospheric venues were former theatres – Corona Theatre, La Tulipe, Le National and L'Olympia. More contemporary joints include as MTELUS and Club Soda in the in the Quartier des spectacles.

Théâtre Fairmount hosts well-known international acts, while Upstairs Jazz Bar & Grill and Le Balcon specialize in live jazz, blues and soul. Expect more edgy performances at Le Ritz PDB, l'Escogriffe Bar Spectacle and Turbo Haüs.

Cirque du Soleil performance

THEATRE AND CULTURAL PERFORMANCE

Montréal's astoundingly varied theatre, music, dance and art – and its formidable festival season – centres on the Quartier des Spectacles (www.quartier desspectacles.com). Dubbed the "Broadway of Montréal", it has over 80 cultural venues and hosts more than 40 festivals.

The world-famous Cirque du Soleil (www.cirquedusoleil.com) is headquartered in Montréal, and though it doesn't feature a permanent show, the circus generally performs in late spring and early summer in the Vieux-Port, where it erects its famous blue-and-yellow tents. Montréal also has numerous excellent dance troupes, from Les Grands Ballets Canadiens (https://grandsballets.com/en) to Les Ballets Jazz de Montréal (www.bjmdanse.ca).

In Québec City the main performances venue is the Grand Théâtre de Québec (https://grandtheatre.qc.ca), home to the L'Orchestre symphonique de Québec (www.osq.org). The Théâtre Capitole (www.lecapitole.com) hosts a wide variety of shows. Smaller venues include Théâtre Periscope (https://m.theatreperiscope.qc.ca) and Théâtre Petit-Champlain (www.theatrepetitchamplain.com).

The Théâtre du Cégep de Trois-Rivières (www.cultur3r.com) proves that there's plenty of cultural life beyond the big cities; Théâtre Granada (https://theatre granada.com) is a great place for shows in Sherbrooke, while Rivière-du-Loup has the Centre Culturel Berger (www.rdlen spectacles.com). Tadoussac has Théâtre des Béloufilles (https://theatredesbelou filles.com), and Sept-Îles has the Salle de Spectacle Jean-Marc-Dion (www.salle jmd.com).

Comedy

Montréal has a dynamic live comedy scene, with regular shows and events at the Montreal Comedy Club (https://mtlcomedyclub.com), the Comedy Nest (https://comedynest.com), and the ComedyVille (www.comedyville.ca). Montréal also hosts the annual Just for Laughs (www.hahaha.com/en), festival.

LGBTQ Montréal

Montréal has a thriving LGBTQ scene, with the action concentrated in the area known as The Village – roughly located on rue Ste-Catherine est between rue Amherst and the Papineau Métro station. Fugues (www.fugues.com) is one of the city's main monthly French LGBTQ magazines and websites. In early August, Divers Cité (http://diverscite.org), the pride parade, is the event of the year, while in October the massive Black & Blue circuit party (http://bbcm.org) is one of the city's – if not Canada's – biggest and wildest LGBTQ parties. Most of the restaurants and hangouts in The Village cater to an LGBTQ crowd in the evening, but are more mixed during the day.

Kayaking on river in Laurentians

OUTDOOR ACTIVITIES

With vast swathes of virgin forest, jagged mountains, wild rivers and a massive coastline, outdoor adventure is easy to find in Québec, with hiking, sailing, canoeing and skiing in some of the most beautiful surroundings in the world.

Québec's mountains, lakes, rivers and forests offer the opportunity to indulge in a vast range of outdoor pursuits, from rock climbing to stand-up paddleboarding. The most popular activities are hiking, kayaking, skiing and cycling, much of this taking place in the region's sensational national parks, of which there are 24 altogether. In terms of spectator sports, NHL's Montreal Canadiens reign supreme, with a record 25 championships, but there are several other professional sports teams playing in Canadian national or regional leagues.

OUTDOOR ACTIVITIES

Québec's national parks are prime targets for outdoor activities, especially hiking, camping and kayaking. All of the national and provincial parks in Québec have well-marked and well-maintained trails.

Long-distance hiking trails
Many of the long-distance trails in Québec form part of the Trans Canada Trail (https://thegreattrail.ca). The Traversé de Charlevoix (www.traversee-decharlevoix.qc.ca) is a 105km hut-to-

hut hiking trail from the Parc national de Grands-Jardins (near Baie-Saint-Paul) to Mont Grand-Fonds through Charlevoix's backcountry, while the Les Sentiers de l'Estrie (www.lessentiersdelestrie.qc.ca) runs some 150km from Glen Sutton on the Vermont border to Kingsbury – a pass is required to walk the trails.

Skiing and other winter sports
Québec is a paradise for skiers, with world-class resorts at Mont-Tremblant (www.tremblant.ca), and around Saint-Sauveur-des-Monts (www.sommets.com) in the Laurentians offering a wide-range of winter activities, everything from cross-country skiing to ice-climbing and snowboarding. Other hotpots include Ski Bromont (www.bromontmontagne.com), Stoneham (https://ski-stoneham.com), Mont-Sainte-Anne (https://mont-sainte-anne.com) and Le Massif (www.lemassif.com), which has some of the most spectacular views of any resort in the world.

Tubing, ice-skating and an indoor climbing wall are available at Stoneham, while Mont-Sainte-Anne offers ice-skating, snowshoeing, dog-sledding, paragliding, sleigh-riding and snowmobiling. On the fringes of Québec City at

Snowshoes running with Montréal background

Montmorency Falls is the world's largest ice-climbing school, L'Ascension École d'escalade (https://rocgyms.com).

Cycling and Mountain Biking

Québec has an exceptionally well-developed cycle network, La Route Verte (Green Route; www.routeverte.com). Highlights include the P'tit Train du Nord linear park (https://ptittraindunord.com), a disused railway line, running for 230km north from St-Jérôme to Mont-Laurier, with sweeping mountain vistas along the way. The Petit Témis (http://en.petit-temis.ca) begins in Rivière-du-Loup and ends 134km later in Cabano in the Gaspé Peninsula. The route follows a flat disused railroad bed, which makes for a gentle ride through bucolic countryside. The relatively flat 265km-long Véloroute des Bleuets (https://veloroutedes bleuets.com) encircles the whole of Lac Saint-Jean.

Mountain bikers should check out Mont-Sainte-Anne ski resort in summer, the longest-standing venue on the mountain bike world-cup circuit. The Traversée de Charlevoix trail is also open to mountain bikers (see above).

WATER SPORTS AND ACTIVITIES

Thanks to strong winds in the Gulf of St Lawrence, the Magdalen Islands are an especially big centre for windsurfing and kitesurfing, while sea kayaking is popular around the Rocher Percé (see page 102), Saguenay Fjord (see page 84) and especially in the Mingan archipelago. Whale-watching is big business in the lower St Lawrence; humpback whales, fin whales, right whales, minke whales, and even beluga can be seen over the summer months. Rivière-du-Loup, Percé, Tadoussac and Les Escoumins are the best places to take whale-watching tours.

SPECTATOR SPORTS

Québec is hockey mad, with the National Hockey League founded in Montréal in 1917, and the Montreal Canadiens (Les Canadiens de Montréal; www.nhl.com/canadiens) still the league's most successful team. Watching them play in the Bell Centre is a right of passage and unforgettable experience.

The Montreal Alouettes compete in the Canadian Football League (with games at Percival Molson Memorial Stadium; https://en.montrealalouettes.com), while CF Montréal (www.cf montreal.com) plays Major League Soccer at Saputo Stadium at Olympic Park.

Québec City has the Québec Capitales (Les Capitales de Québec; https://capitalesdequebec.com), a professional baseball team in the Frontier League, playing their homes games at Stade Canac; the Trois-Rivières Aigles (https://lesaiglestr.com) play in the same league. There are currently 12 Québec teams in the Québec Major Junior Hockey League (part of the Canadian Hockey League); the Rouyn-Noranda Huskies won the Memorial Cup in 2019.

BEST ROUTES

Place d'Armes

A WALK IN VIEUX-MONTRÉAL

Vieux–Montréal ("Old Montréal") was where it all started in the 17th century. Today this historic district of cobbled streets, old churches and museums, in between Downtown and the St Lawrence River, makes for an enchanting day of exploration.

DISTANCE: 2.5km
TIME: A full day
START: Place d'Armes
END: Place d'Youville
POINTS TO NOTE: If you're planning to visit the Musée d'Archéologie et d'Histoire de Montréal, avoid doing this walk on a Monday, when it's closed – the Hôtel de Ville is usually closed at weekends. Otherwise most sights and restaurants in this route open daily in the summer (May–Oct); at the other times hours are often limited, so check ahead. Place-d'Armes can be accessed from Métro Line 2 (Place-d'Armes station), while Square-Victoria station (also Line 2) is just 400m from the Customs House at the end of the tour. The tour can be easily completed on foot, and can also be combined (on foot) with the Downtown and Quartier des Spectacles Walk (see page 32). For Montréal accommodation, see page 106.

Home to over a third of all Québécois, the island metropolis of Montréal cele-brates both its European heritage and its reputation as a truly international city. There can be few places in the world where people on the street flit so easily between two or more languages – sometimes within the same sentence – or whose cafés and bars ooze such a cosmopolitan feel. The gracious district now known as Vieux-Montréal ("Old Montréal") was where the colony of Fort Ville-Marie was founded in 1642. The greatest concentration of 17th-, 18th- and 19th-century buildings in North America has its fair share of tourists, but it's popular with Montréalers, too. This tour takes in some of the highlights.

PLACE D'ARMES

Get an early start and make for **Place d'Armes** ❶, the focal point of Vieux-Montréal. Its centre is occupied by a century-old statue of Paul de Cho-medey, Sieur de Maisonneuve, founder of Montréal. The red-sandstone building on the northeast corner of Place d'Armes (at Rue St-Jacques) was built for the New York Life Insurance Co in 1888 and

Château Ramezay   *Interior of the Notre-Dame Basilica*

at eight storeys high, was the city's first skyscraper. Next door, the **Aldred Building** (completed 1931) is one of the finest examples of the Art Deco style in the city. Both are dwarfed today by the black International-style monolith on the south side of the square, a controversial addition to the Vieux-Montréal skyline when it was completed in 1968 as the **Banque Canadienne Nationale Tower** ❸.

Basilique Notre-Dame

Take a look inside the twin-towered, neo-Gothic **Basilique Notre-Dame** ❹ (www.basiliquenotredame.ca; Mon–Fri 8am–4.30pm, Sat 8am–4pm, Sun 12.30–4pm; $10, includes 20min tour), which looms over the eastern side of Place d'Armes. The breathtaking gilt and sky-blue interior, flooded with light from three rose windows unusually set in the ceiling, was designed by Montréal architect Vic-

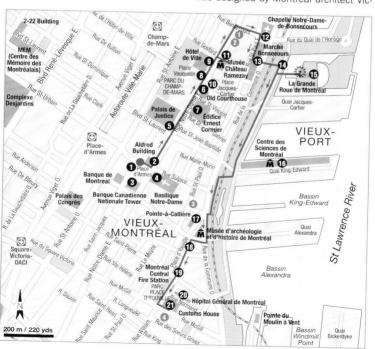

tor Bourgeau. Imported from Limoges in France, the stained glass windows depict the founding of Ville-Marie. Behind the main altar is the **Chapelle Sacré-Coeur**, destroyed by a serious fire in 1978 but rebuilt with an impressive modern bronze reredos by Charles Daudelin.

RUE NOTRE-DAME

From Place d'Armes walk northeast along the city's first street, **Rue Notre-Dame**, laid out in 1672. One block on you'll pass the black glass behemoth of the **Palais de Justice** on the corner of boulevard St-Laurent. It overshadows its forerunner, one block further, the imposing **Old Courthouse** (155 rue Notre-Dame est) erected by the British in 1856. Now known as the **Édifice Lucien-Saulnier**, since 2019 it has served as a temporary City Hall (until 2022) while the original is renovated. Criminal trials once took place across the street, at 100 rue Notre-Dame est, in the **Édifice Ernest Cormier** , completed in 1926, and now the Québec Court of Appeal.

PLACE VAUQUELIN

The Old Courthouse borders **Place Vauquelin** , centred on a pretty fountain and statue of the French 18th-century naval commander Jean Vauquelin. Digging to build a car park here hit rock, which turned out to be the original city walls; they were excavated, restored, and the area made into a pleasant grassy space instead, with **Parc du Champ-de-Mars** just to the northwest.

Hôtel de Ville
The north side of Place Vauquelin is dominated by the highly ornate **Hôtel de Ville** , Montréal's City Hall (http://ville.montreal.qc.ca; Mon–Fri 8am–5pm; 45min guided tours hourly in summer Mon–Fri 11am–4pm; free), which should be open again by the summer of 2022 after a three-year renovation. The areas open to visitors include the Council Chamber and the Hall of Honour.

PLACE JACQUES-CARTIER

A popular gathering spot for locals and tourists, the lively, cobbled **Place Jacques-Cartier** , originally built as a market in 1804, slopes down towards the river from Place Vauquelin. The square is filled with outdoor restaurants and cafés, along with buskers, street artists and caricaturists. At the top of the square itself looms the controversial Colonne Nelson or **Nelson's Column**. The city's oldest monument was funded by anglophone Montréalers delighted with Nelson's 1805 defeat of the French at Trafalgar. One block further along Notre-Dame is the absorbing Musée Château Ramezay.

MUSÉE CHÂTEAU RAMEZAY

The long and low fieldstone manor of the **Musée Château Ramezay** (280 rue Notre-Dame est; www.chateauramezay.

Tulips in front of the Hotel de Ville

qc.ca; June–Nov daily 9.30am–6pm; Dec–May Tue–Sun 10am–4.30pm; $11), set in stately gardens, features a collection of oil paintings, domestic arte-facts, tools, costumes and furniture from the 18th and 19th centuries. Keep walk-ing northeast along Notre-Dame for one block to **Muru Crêpe** (see ❶) for a tasty lunch, and/or a superb coffee at adja-cent **Café de' Mercanti** (see ❷).

CHAPELLE NOTRE-DAME-DE-BONSECOURS

After lunch walk down cobbled Rue Bonsecours to the delicate and pro-fusely steepled **Chapelle Notre-Dame-de-Bonsecours** ⑫ (400 rue St-Paul est; https://margueritebourgeoys.org; Mar–Apr and early Sept to early Jan Tue–Sun 11am–4pm; May to early Sept daily 10am–6pm; chapel free; museum $12), or the "Sailors' Church", at the bottom of the hill. The chapel dates back to the 1650s, under the instigation of **Marguerite Bourgeoys**, who founded the nation's first religious order and was in charge of the "filles du Roi" – young French women who immigrated to marry bachelor settlers and multiply the pop-ulation of the colony. She became Can-ada's first saint in 1982. The chapel also contains the small **Musée Mar-guerite-Bourgeoys** devoted to her life, as well as temporary exhibits on early explorers, missionaries and traders. The entry price lets you climb the nar-row stairs leading to the summit of the

Get festive

Montréal explodes with festivals in the summer, many taking place in the enter-tainment quarter, Quartier des Spec-tacles. For festival news and updates, consult www.mtl.org/en. The world-re-nowned Cirque du Soleil (www.cirque-dusoleil.com), based in Montréal, also regularly puts on shows.
International Fireworks Competition June and July www.laronde.com/laron-deen/linternational-des-feux/overview. Breathtaking, music-coordinated pyro-technics at La Ronde amusement park on Île Sainte-Hélène.
Francofolies Mid-June www.francos montreal.com. Brings French musicians from around the world to various down-town stages.
Festival International de Jazz de Mon-tréal Late June and early July https:// montrealjazzfest.com. Largest jazz event in North America, with mostly free shows at huge open-air stages in the Quartier des Spectacles.
Montréal First Peoples' Festival July www.presenceautochtone.ca/en. A lively event celebrating Aboriginal peoples' his-tory and featuring traditional activities, from throat-singing to stonecutting.
Juste pour Rire ("Just For Laughs") Mid-July www.hahaha.com/en. The largest comedy festival in the world.
Festival International Nuits d'Afrique July www.festivalnuitsdafrique.com. The sounds of African beats fill the city.

tower above the apse, where the "aerial chapel" gives sweeping views.

RUE ST-PAUL

The chapel stands on **Rue St-Paul**, one of Montréal's most attractive thoroughfares. Take a look inside the **Marché Bonsecours**, just to the south of the chapel.

Marché Bonsecours

The striking, silver-domed **Marché Bonsecours ⓑ** (https://marchebonsecours. qc.ca; see website for seasonal hours), built in the mid-19th century, sparkles over Vieux-Montréal. For years this elegant building was used for municipal offices, but for the city's 350th birthday in 1992 it was restored and transformed to house restaurants, boutiques, and a number of shops specializing in Québécois crafts, leatherwork, jewellery, antiques and artwork. You can also pick up local delicacies, including a huge variety of maple products (syrup, candles, tea), ice cider and more.

VIEUX-PORT

Exit the Marché Bonsecours on the east side and you'll be in the heart of the **Vieux-Port ⓮** district, once the principal import and export conduit of the continent. The Vieux-Port comes into its own in the summer, with a variety of festivals and activities, including an outdoor film festival, obstacle courses and cir-

cus and trapeze acts. Head towards the water then stroll south along the promenade; families may want to check out **La Grande Roue de Montréal ⓯** (www. lagranderouedemontreal.com; daily 11am–11pm; $25.87), a 60-metre high observation wheel with sensational views, or the kid-friendly **Centre des Sciences de Montréal ⓰** (www.centre-dessciencesdemontreal.com; Mon–Fri 9am–4pm, Sat–Sun 9am–5pm; $22), further south on Kind Edward Quay. At King Edward Quay, leave the promenade and walk west over to Place Royale.

MUSÉE D'ARCHÉOLOGIE ET D'HISTOIRE DE MONTRÉAL

Once the site of duels, whippings and public hangings amid the peddlers and hawkers who sold wares from the incoming ships, tiny **Place Royale** is dominated by the neat classical facade of the 1830s **Old Customs House** and **Pointe-à-Callière ⓱** (https://pacmusee. qc.ca; Tue–Fri 10am–5pm, Sat–Sun 11am–5pm; $24), the Montreal Archaeology and History Complex. The museum stands on the site where the first French settlers came ashore in 1642, a point on the river known as "Pointe-à-Callière". The sleek, superbly curated museum, which spreads underground below Place Royale and includes the Old Customs House, focuses on the development of Montréal as a meeting and trading place, as told through the archeological remains excavated here at the old

est part of the city, as well as high-tech audiovisual presentations. If you fancy a break, grab a coffee and pastry at **Maison Christian Faure** (see ❸).

PLACE D'YOUVILLE

End your tour at **Place d'Youville** ⓲ behind the Pointe-à-Callière museum, where the **Monument aux Pionniers** obelisk commemorates the city founders. This portion of the square was renamed **Place de la Grande-Paix** in 2001, to mark the tercentennial of the Great Peace of Montréal, a treaty signed here in 1701 to end the conflict between the Indigenous and French settlers. As you stroll south look out for the old **Montréal Central Fire Station** ⓳, built in a lavish Flemish style in 1904. At Rue Saint-Pierre, walk a little to see the old walls of the **Hôpital Général de Montréal** ⓴ which dates back to 1694. Back on Place d'Youville, the grand building on the corner of Rue McGill is the Beaux-Arts **Customs House** ㉑, completed in 1916 and featured in the 2001 De Niro movie *The Score*. End the day with meal at **Restaurant Pastel** (see ❹), across the street at 124 rue McGill.

Food and Drink

❶ MURU CRÊPE

362 rue Notre-Dame Est; tel: 514-759 6755; www.facebook.com/murucrepe; Tue–Sun 9am–3pm; $

Modern lunch spot specializing in crêpes, from savoury versions with smoked salmon, goat cheese and mushrooms, and chicken, to sweet versions with maple syrup, s'mores, and fresh berries.

❷ CAFÉ DE' MERCANTI

350 rue Notre-Dame Est; tel: 514-569 7620; https://cafedemercanti.com; daily 7.30am–5pm; $

Italian-owned coffee specialist that knocks our excellent espresso with blends made in-house, as well as croissants, pastries and cookies, including gluten-free options.

❸ MAISON CHRISTIAN FAURE

355 place Royale; tel: 514-508 6453; https://maisonchristianfaure.ca; daily 9am–6pm; $

Excellent patisserie in sleek, contemporary digs serving exquisite éclairs, macaroons, mille-feuilles and madeleines, as well as Illy brand coffee, a variety of teas, and a celebrated hot chocolate.

❹ RESTAURANT PASTEL

124 rue McGill; tel: 514-395 9015; www.resto pastel.com; Tue–Sat 11.30am–10pm; $$

This spacious restaurant with exposed brick walls daubed with light, pastel colours was opened by Kabir Kapoor and chef Jason Morris to general acclaim in 2018. It's best known for its nine-course seasonal tasting menus, but a la carte dishes range from lobster ravioli to honey cake.

MONTRÉAL: DOWNTOWN AND QUARTIER DES SPECTACLES

Downtown Montréal blends glass and steel skyscrapers with leafy boulevards. The adjacent Quartier des Spectacles serves as Montréal's cultural hub, booming with performing arts venues, lively restaurants and outdoor public spaces and walkways.

DISTANCE: 3.5km
TIME: A full day
START: Square Dorchester
END: MEM (Centre des Mémoire des Montréalais)
POINTS TO NOTE: If you're planning to visit the museums and churches, avoid doing this walk on a Monday, when some are closed. Otherwise, most sights and restaurants open daily in the summer (May–Oct); check ahead for other months. Square Dorchester and MEM can be accessed from Métro Line 2 (Bonaventure and Champ-de-Mars stations respectively). The tour can be completed on foot, though several buses shuttle up and down Rue Ste-Catherine (see www.stm.info) – single fares are $3.50 (exact change required). This tour can also be combined (on foot) with the Vieux-Montréal route. For Montréal accommodation, see page 106.

Downtown is where Canada's second-largest city is at its most international. Its skyline of glass and concrete rises above churches and monuments in a melange of European styles as varied as Montréal's social mix. Here, the boulevards and leafy squares buzz from the morning rush hour right through to the early hours, when clubbers return from Rue Ste-Catherine and the Plateau and Quartier Latin districts. Of the main streets, Rue Ste-Catherine offers the most in the way of shopping, dining and entertainment. The Quartier des Spectacles functions as Montréal's entertainment hub, home to numerous theatres, performance centres and the MEM museum. Montréal prides itself as a winter destination; their RÉSO system is essentially an underground city, some 32km of climate-controlled tunnels and subterranean malls, allowing visitors to navigate their way safely around during harsher weather.

SQUARE DORCHESTER

Start the day at **Square Dorchester** ❶, right in the centre of downtown and a good spot to get your bearings. The space opened in 1878, on land that was once a cemetery (look for small crosses

Montréal's downtown

embedded in the pathways as a tribute), and was originally known as Dominion Square. The Art Deco-inspired **Dominion Square Building**, raised in 1930 on the northwest side of the square, is home to the *Montreal Gazette*, the site of the Infotouriste office and the starting point for various guided tours; there are also

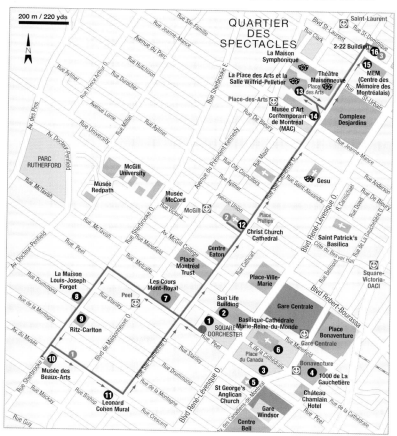

Barbie Expo at Les Cours Mont-Royal

occasional lunchtime concerts here in summer. The vast **Sun Life Building** ❷ dominates the northeast side, but is now dwarfed by the **CIBC Tower** opposite, a 187 metre-tall skyscraper. The four main monuments on the square are the Wilfrid Laurier Memorial, the Boer War Memorial, the Robert Burns Memorial, and the "Lion of Belfort", a British Imperial Lion inspired by Frédéric Bartholdi's giant lion sculpture in France.

The southeastern half of the square across René-Lévesque Boulevard was dubbed **Place du Canada** ❸ during the 1967 centennial. Looming over this end is **1000 de la Gauchetière** ❹, Montréal's tallest building (at 205m), and the similarly tall Château Champlain Hotel, opened in the late 1960s.

St George's Anglican Church

Wander over to the southeastern side of Place du Canada to view the area's oldest building, **St George's Anglican Church** ❺ (www.st-georges.org; Tue–Fri 9am–4pm, Sat–Sun 9am–3pm). Completed in 1870, its solid neo-Gothic sandstone exterior gives way to a lofty interior, where trusses that rise in a series of arches support the double hammer-beam roof; check out the striking stained glass windows.

Basilique-Cathédrale Marie-Reine-du-Monde

On the other side of Place du Canada, the **Basilique-Cathédrale Marie-Reine-du-Monde** ❻ (Mon–Fri 7am–7pm, Sat–Sun 7.30am–7pm) was commissioned by Bishop Ignace Bourget in 1875 as a scaled-down replica of Rome's famous St Peter's Basilica. To your left on entering, the **Chapelle des Souvenirs** contains various relics, including the wax-encased remains of St Zoticus, a patron saint of the poor.

LES COURS MONT-ROYAL

Leave Square Dorchester on Rue Peel, heading northwest, and in a couple of blocks you'll reach elegant **Les Cours Mont-Royal** ❼ (1455 rue Peel; https://lcmr.ca; Mon–Wed 10am–6pm, Thu–Fri 10am–7pm, Sat 10am–5pm, Sun noon–5pm). Formerly the largest hotel in the British Commonwealth, it now contains four floors of shops, along with spas and a high-end food court, all topped by apartments and offices. **Barbie Expo** (http://expobarbie.ca; Mon–Wed 9am–8pm, Thu–Fri 9am–10pm, Sat 9am–6pm, Sun 9am–5pm; free), the largest permanent exhibit of Barbie dolls in the world, is also on view here, featuring dolls dressed by leading designers, including Christian Dior, Oscar de la Renta and Ralph Lauren. From here it's a 10-minute walk along Peel, then south along Rue Sherbrooke to the Museum of Fine Arts.

GOLDEN SQUARE MILE

On route to the art museum, there are a couple of sights to look out for on **Rue Sherbrooke**. **La Maison Louis-Joseph**

Leonard Cohen mural

Montreal Boer War Memorial

Forget ❽ (no. 1195) is a stately mansion built for the affluent Forget family in 1884 in Second Empire style. With the neighbouring Reid-Wilson House (no. 1201, built 1882) and still prestigious Mount Royal Club (built in 1906 by McKim, Mead & White), it's one of the last vestiges of the city's vaunted **Golden Square Mile** along Sherbrooke. This upscale, primarily Anglophone neighbourhood flourished between 1850 and 1930, home to some of Canada's richest families and "commercial aristocracy" of the city. On the other side of the street, one block down, is the **Ritz-Carlton** ❾, the most glamorous hotel in Montréal.

MUSÉE DES BEAUX-ARTS

Aim to spend the rest of the morning in the superb **Musée des Beaux-Arts** ❿ (1380 rue Sherbrooke Ouest; www.mbam.qc.ca; Tue–Sun 10am–5pm, main exhibits Wed till 8pm; $24, $16 ages 21 to 30, Wed night $12), Canada's oldest museum – and Montréal's largest – featuring the most impressive Canadian art collection in the country. You could spend several days exploring the six major sections in the five pavilions of the museum complex, but with around two hours, it is possible to see some of the highlights.

Michal and Renata Hornstein Pavilion for Peace

First, head to the **Michal and Renata Hornstein Pavilion for Peace**, which showcases international art by Matisse, Renoir, Cézanne, Holbein, Monet, Poussin and all the Old Masters. Look out for Rodin's sensuous sculpture *Sirens*, Rembrandt's *Portrait of a Young Woman* and Toulouse-Lautrec's *Babylone d'Allemagne*. On Level 2, don't miss the **Napoleon Gallery**, which contains a rare collection of Napoleon Bonaparte related paintings, sculpture and artefacts.

Claire and Marc Bourgie Pavilion

The dazzling marble-and-glass **Claire and Marc Bourgie Pavilion** was built in 2011 as an extension of the restored Erskine and American Church, and is as impressive as the art within. There's remarkable Inuit Art on Level 4, and the Canadian Modernists on Level 1. It also displays the church's 18 Tiffany stained glass windows, the largest collection of Tiffany's work outside the US. Finally, have a quick stroll around the **CGI Sculpture Garden**. There are places to eat in the museum, but for hearty Caribbean food, leave and walk down Crescent Street to **Lloydie's Crescent** (see ❶).

RUE STE-CATHERINE

As you walk along Crescent Street you'll see the city's beloved **Leonard Cohen Mural** ⓫ (northwest on the side of 1420 Crescent St). When you hit **Rue Ste-Catherine**, turn left (northeast). The city's main commercial thoroughfare since the early 1900s, Rue Ste-Catherine stretches for 12km

across the island, with the part east of Rue Guy serving as the main shopping artery. It's just under a kilometre stroll to Christ Church Cathedral, but you can also hop on bus #15 or #358 (from Sainte-Catherine/de la Montagne to Sainte-Catherine/Robert-Bourassa).

Christ Church Cathedral

The quiet grounds of the 1859 Anglican **Christ Church Cathedral** 🔵 (635 rue Ste-Catherine Ouest; www.montreal cathedral.ca; daily 8am–6pm) provide a welcome break in the commercial strip of Rue Ste-Catherine. The cathedral leased all the land around and beneath the church, and was supported on concrete struts while the developers tunnelled out the glitzy **Promenades de la Cathédrale**, a boutique-lined part of the Underground City. Grab a coffee at **Café Olimpico** (see ②) behind the church, then continue walking along Rue Ste-Catherine – it's around half a kilometre to La Place des Arts.

La Place des Arts

Dubbed as the "Broadway of Montréal", **La Place des Arts** 🔵 (https://placedes arts.com) forms the core of the **Quartier des Spectacles** (www.quartierdes spectacles.com), home to the Montreal Symphony Orchestra, the Orchestre Métropolitain, Les Grands Ballets Canadiens, and the Opéra de Montréal. There are over 40 performance spaces and hosts more than 40 festivals. On the south side of La Place des Arts (on Rue Jeanne Mance), the **Place des Festivals** opened in 2009, hosting most of the bigger festivals, and featuring the largest animated fountains in Canada, with 235 water jets and four massive lighting towers.

Musée d'Art Contemporain de Montréal (MAC)

Occupying the west side of the Place des Arts, the **Musée d'Art Contemporain de Montréal** 🔵 (185 rue Ste-Catherine Ouest; https://macm.org; Tue 11am–6pm, Wed–Fri 11am–9pm, Sat–Sun

---

Griffintown

Griffintown, in the southwest of Montréal, was once the domain of Irish labourers – now, it's one of Montréal's hippest residential neighbourhoods. An ever-growing array of design shops, fashion retailers, restaurants and bars cater to the neighbourhood's new demographic. At the heart is the Centre d'Art de Montréal (Montréal Art Centre; 1844 rue William; www.montrealartcenter.com; Mon–Sat 11am–5pm, Sun 11am–3pm). This community arts centre features a variety of exhibits by local artists, and also runs the popular Griffintown Art School, with workshops and classes in all forms of art, from sculpture to ceramics to painting. L'Arsenal (2020 rue William; www.arsenalcontemporary.com; Wed–Fri 10am–6pm, Sat 10am–5pm; $10), housed in a former shipyard, also occasionally hosts exhibits.

Musée d'Art Contemporain

10am–6pm; \$15) is the first museum in Canada devoted entirely to contemporary art. It showcases Québécois artists and works by other Canadian and international artists. The daring temporary exhibits are consistently excellent.

MEM (Centre des Mémoire des Montréalais)

Explore multimedia exhibits of the city's history at the engaging **MEM (Centre des Mémoire des Montréalais ⓯**; https://memmtl.ca), the old Center d'histoire de Montréal, which should open in 2022 in new digs at the corner of Rue Ste-Catherine and Boulevard Saint-Laurent, a short walk from the contemporary art museum. Daily life in the early days of Montréal will be evoked via films, period furnishings and crafts, as well as citizens' voices, past and present. If it's not yet open check out the stylish **2-22 Building ⓰** across the street, designed by Ædifica and Gilles Huot Architectes. It houses nine different cultural and community venues, including **La Vitrine Culturelle** ("the Cultural Window"; 2 rue Sainte-Catherine Est; Sun–Mon 11am–6pm, Tue–Sat 11am–8pm), a tech-savvy information and ticket centre with the city's most extensive information on arts and entertainment offerings. If you haven't already, check out what's on offer this evening; the same building houses **Accord - Le Bistro** (see ❸), a refined spot for dinner.

Food and Drink

❶ LLOYDIE'S CRESCENT

2145 Crescent St; tel: 514-849 5858; https://lloydies.ca; Mon–Sat 11.30am–10pm; \$

Best Caribbean food in Montréal, with Jamaican classics such as jerk chicken, oxtail, jerk pork, fried chicken and veggies served with rice, plantain and coconut coleslaw. Also celebrated for its Jamaican patties, stewed pies and mac pie.

❷ CAFÉ OLIMPICO

1333 blvd Robert-Bourassa; https://cafe olimpico.com; Mon–Fri 8am–5pm, Sat–Sun 11am–5pm; \$

Local mini coffee house chain with three branches in the city, and truly stellar Italian-style espresso and Italian pastries. It's been around since 1970, but this branch in the old Presbytery behind the cathedral has a classy, modern feel.

❸ ACCORDS - LE BISTRO

22 rue Sainte-Catherine Est; tel: 514-508 2122; www.facebook.com/accordsbistro; Tue–Sat 3–11pm; \$\$

Elegant French bistro with changing menus that might start with Arctic char tartine, feature parmesan gnocchi with artichokes, Québec fish or Québec veal shoulder, and end with beignets, lemon madeleines or chocolate tarts.

THE LAURENTIANS

Looming mightily on the north side of the St Lawrence, the Laurentians are one of the oldest mountain ranges in the world. Get a taster of the vast interior of Québec on this three day road-trip taking in pioneer villages, thrilling ski resorts and old covered bridges.

DISTANCE: 325km
TIME: 3 days
START: Montréal
END: Mount Laurier
POINTS TO NOTE: This tour is designed as a road-trip – cars are easy to rent. At its southern end the route can be extended with the walking tours around Montréal (see pages 26 and 32) and the road trips through the wine region (see page 44) and Centre-du-Québec (see page 54). The route has been primarily designed for spring, summer and fall travel – although many sights on the route close completely or partially from September to May, the roads are usually open year-round and much of the region comes alive with winter sports and activities at that time; for information on the Laurentides region, visit www.laurentides.com. The main regional tourist office lies just off Autoroute 15 (exit 51) in the Porte-du-Nord Rest Area (tel: 450-224 7007), just north of Saint-Jérôme. For accommodation options see page 107.

The Laurentides administrative region of Québec only encompasses a portion of the Laurentian Mountains, which run from the Ottawa River all the way to Labrador. It boasts a rippling landscape of undulating hills and valleys, and a vast sweep of coniferous forest dotted with hundreds of tranquil lakes and rivers. The construction of the P'tit Train du Nord railway between 1891 and 1909 opened the region to the mining and lumber industries, but today it's one of the largest ski areas in North America, helmed by the esteemed Mont-Tremblant. The train tracks have been replaced by a terrific 232km cycling trail, the Parc Linéaire Le P'tit Train du Nord. This tour follows the "Route des Belles-Histoires" from Saint-Jérôme to Mont-Laurier, along Rte-117 and Autoroute 15, up the Rivière du Nord valley, tracing the route of the early colonists and the pioneering railway.

DAY 1: SAINT-JÉRÔME

Though its 60km from downtown Montréal, **Saint-Jérôme ❶** is the gateway to the Laurentians. Head to the **Cathédrale**

Mont–Tremblant village

Saint-Jérôme (355 place du Curé-La-belle; daily 9am–noon and 1–4pm; free) in the centre of town, a handsome pile built in the 1890s and indelibly linked to Roman Catholic priest Antoine Labelle (1833–1891). Labelle was the priest in Saint-Jérôme from 1868 until his death, but he's mainly remembered for championing the construction of the Le P'tit Train du Nord railway and encouraging settlement of the Rivière du Nord valley. Learn all about the "King of the North" at the **Curé Labelle Exhibition Space** inside the cathedral.

SAINT-SAUVEUR

Just 20km north of **Saint-Jérôme** via Autoroute 15, **Saint-Sauveur ❷** is surrounded by ski resorts popular with Montréal day-trippers. The main drag, Rue Principale, is lined with restaurants, shops and boutiques, while the **Musée du Ski des Laurentides** (30 av Filion; https://museeduski.com; Wed–Sun 11am–6pm; free) is a good place to learn about the history of winter sports in the region. Under "Les Sommets" (www.sommets.com) umbrella, there are five ski resorts altogether, 156 trails and six ski schools. The closest resort, just south of town, is **Sommet Saint-Sauveur,** which transforms into an amusement and water park in the summer, with plenty of trails for hikers and mountain bikers. Grab lunch in town at **Lou Smoked Meat** (see ❶); the best place for a coffee is **Café White Et Compagnie** (see ❷).

VAL-DAVID

Continue north on Autoroute 15 and Rte-117 for 22km to **Val-David ❸**, the vaguely bohemian resort of the Laurentians. The main street, **Rue de l'Église**, has galleries and shops, many run by the artisans themselves, and the village thrums with energy during the popular midsummer festival **1001 Pots** (https://1001pots.com). The **Centre d'Exposition de Val-David** (2495 rue de l'Église; www.culture.val-david.qc.ca; see website for seasonal hours; free) features temporary exhibits, from painting to photography to sculpture. The local tourist office is housed in the old station, **La Petite Gare**, nearby on the P'tit Train du Nord bicycle path. Val-David is a good place to spend the night (see page 107), with **La Table des Gourmets** (see ❸) a superb choice for dinner. If you have time, and it's still light, check out the easy hiking trails just outside town in the maple woods of **Parc Régional de Val-David-Val-Morin ❹** (www.parcregional.com; $8–12).

DAY 2: SAINTE-AGATHE-DES-MONTS

The historic downtown of **Sainte-Agathe-des-Monts ❺** lies just 7km west from Val-David, on the shores of **Lac de Sables**. Once the railway had arrived here in 1892 the town took off as a wellness retreat, and by 1910 it was crammed with the summer homes of Montréal's

Sainte-Agathe-des-Monts Church in the Fal...

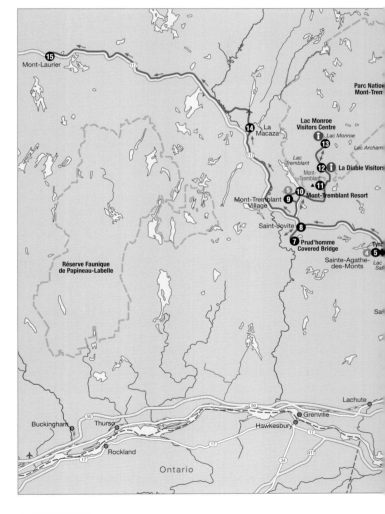

Mont–Tremblant Lake sunrise

movers and shakers. Grab breakfast at **Couleur Café Signature** (see ④) before having a quick peek at the 19th-century Laurentien Store (on the corner of Rue Principale and Rue Saint-Vincent) built by Montréal's Forget family in 1897 (now a restaurant). Further along Rue Principale Est, the impressive twin-towered Romanesque church, **Eglise Sainte-Agathe**, was completed in 1905. Make a stop at **Tyroparc** ⑥ (www.tyroparc.com) before leaving down, which boasts a massive zipline and via ferrata.

PRUD'HOMME COVERED BRIDGE

It's 30km to the Saint-Jovite sector of Mont-Tremblant from Sainte-Agathe, but it's worth making a 5km detour south on Rte-327 to **Prud'homme Covered Bridge** ⑦, a red-painted wooden structure over the Rivière du Diable, built in 1918 in lush farmland.

MONT-TREMBLANT

Québec's most famous resort has its roots in a community established by the indefatigable Curé Labelle in 1872. Today the city of **Mont-Tremblant** comprises several districts; the **Saint-Jovite** ⑧ sector (aka "Centre-Ville Mont-Tremblant") just off Rte-117; **Mont-Tremblant Village** ⑨, 11km north on Rte-327, which developed on the shores of Lac Mercier after the railway arrived in 1904; and **Mont-Tremblant Resort** ⑩ (www.tremblant.ca), which emerged in the

Mont–Tremblant in the fall

1930s in the shadow of 875-metre high **Mont-Tremblant ⑪** itself, 5km further up on the shores of Lac Tremblant. Aim to spend the rest of the day and night here (see page 107 for accommodation).

Mont-Tremblant Village

Stop for lunch at **Pub Mont-Tremblant-Microbrasserie Baril Roulant** (see ⑤), in the pedestrian-only Mont-Tremblant Village, which has the feel of a Québécois "toy village" and is dotted with ritzy boutiques, cute little walkways and après-ski bars. The pub is opposite the **Place de la Gare**, the reconstructed station, now used as an art gallery (Thu–Mon 10am–5pm; free).

Mont-Tremblant Resort

The premier ski hub of Québec, the **Mont-Tremblant Resort** is now a year-round destination, with a range of activities on offer in summer and the surrounding forests creating incredible colours in the fall. Also known as "Old-Tremblant", many of the buildings here were built in the late 1930s, inspired by the traditional Québec architecture of Île d'Orléans. The lower section of the village is connected to the main upper area by the **Cabriolet**, an open-air gondola. Once up here you can organize a variety of activities, or take the **Télécabine Panoramique** (from $23) cable car to the summit of Mont-Tremblant, where there's a café at the **Grand Manitou** chalet, the **360° Observation Tower**, and a range

of trails through the mountains. Back in the village, take a cruise around **Lac Tremblant** with Croisières Mont-Tremblant (www.croisierestremblant.com).

Parc National du Mont-Tremblant

Spend the afternoon hiking in the **Parc National du Mont-Tremblant** (www.sepaq.com/pq/mot/index.dot?language_id=1; $8.90), a vast wilderness area that spreads northwards from the ski resort. It's a winding 20km from Mont-Tremblant Resort to **La Diable Visitors Centre ⑫** on Chemin du Lac Supérieur, and another 14km up to the main **Lac Monroe Visitors Centre ⑬** – both can provide information about trails and canoeing.

DAY 3: LA MACAZA

Begin day three with a visit to the charming village of **La Macaza ⑭**, 37km northwest of Mont-Tremblant Resort. On the way you'll pass the old **covered bridge** over the Macaza River, built in 1904. In the village itself is the church, built in 1903, and a fabulous fresco in the Hôtel de Ville which depicts the history of the region. It's also worth a peek inside the **Maison de la Culture de La Macaza**, the former studio and residence of artist Jeane Fabb (1950–2013).

MONT-LAURIER

It's another 72km on Rte-117 to **Mont-Laurier ⑮** on the banks of the

Tremblant skiers

Mont–Tremblant village

Lièvre River. Known as the "Capital of the Haute-Laurentides", it marks the northern end of the Laurentides region. In the centre of town stands the **Cathédrale de Mont-Laurier**, but the pride and joy of the town is the **L'Espace Théâtre** (543 rue du Pont; www.espace theatre.com). End your Laurentian journey with a performance at this stylish contemporary theatre.

Food and Drink

1 LOU SMOKED MEAT

17 av de l'Église, Saint-Sauveur; tel: 450-744 0766; www.lousmokedmeat.com; Tue–Sun 11am–7.30pm; $

Small but justly popular lunch stop in a century-old wooden cottage, with a few tables on the porch overlooking Mont Saint-Sauveur. Enjoy various smoked meat sandwiches or plates, poutines, wraps and salads, washed down with a decent range of local beers.

2 CAFÉ WHITE ET COMPAGNIE

31 av de la Gare, Saint-Sauveur; tel: 450-227 0330; www.whiteetcompagnie.com; Tue–Sun 8am–4pm; $

Stylish coffee shop in Saint-Sauveur, opened by a local Québécoise and expat New Zealander, where you can order espresso (sourced from Pilot Coffee Roasters in Toronto), real flat whites, teas from Camélia Sinensis in Montréal and a variety of pastries and light lunches.

3 LA TABLE DES GOURMETS

2353 rue de l'Église, Val-David; tel: 819-322 2353; https://tabledesgourmets.com; Thu–Sun 5–9pm; $$$

Upscale French restaurant which utilizes seasonal and local produce to create fabulous dishes – think local trout, bison and duck, with seared foie gras, oysters, scallops and incredible desserts, including a coffee tiramisu.

4 COULEUR CAFÉ SIGNATURE

7 rue Principale Est, Sainte-Agathe-des-Monts; tel: 819-326 7723; https://couleurcafe.ca; Tue–Sat 7.30am–5pm; $

Contemporary coffee house with minimal décor and long wooden tables that roasts its own blends and serves a tasty selection of snacks, sandwiches, quinoa salad, waffles, pastries and cakes (especially good hazelnut and chocolate mousse cake).

5 PUB DE TREMBLANT-MICROBRASSERIE BARIL ROULANT

1885 chemin du Village, Mont-Tremblant; tel: 819-429 5050; www.barilroulant.com; Thu–Sun 5–9pm; $$

Outlet of a local mini-chain of pubs attached to Val-David's Baril Roulant craft brewery, offering excellent pizzas and small plates (samosas, nachos, salads) in addition to the beers, from HopSession IPA to La Picole honey beer.

LA ROUTE DES VINS

Sip your way through Québec's Cantons-de-l'Est (Eastern Townships) on the "Route des Vins", taking in the region's lush vineyards, ice wine and ice cider producers, cheese makers, small farming towns, clapboard churches, old mills and museums.

DISTANCE: 300km

TIME: 3 days

START/END: Montréal

POINTS TO NOTE: This tour is designed as a road-trip loop from Montréal. The route can be extended with the walking tours around Montréal (see pages 26 and 32), the road trips to through the Laurentians (see page 38) and Centre-du-Québec (see page 54). The route has been primarily designed for spring, summer and fall travel – although many sights on the route close completely or partially from September to May, the roads themselves are usually open year-round and much of the region comes alive with winter sports and activities at that time. The main tourist information centres on route are the Dunham Tourist Office (3809 rue Principale; www.ville.dunham.qc.ca), Cowansville Tourist Office (225 rue Principale, www.ville.cowansville.qc.ca), and Bromont Tourist Office (15 blvd de Bromont, http://tourismebromont.com). For accommodation options see page 108.

The Cantons-de-l'Est (Eastern Townships) were once the quietest corner of Québec, with swaying fields and farmland punctuated by time-capsule villages founded by British Loyalists escaping the American Revolution.

Today, these settlements – many spruced up with luxury inns, art galleries and antique shops – have since become a readily accessible country getaway for Montréalers. Yet the agricultural roots of the region are still evident, especially in spring, when the maple trees are tapped for the sap (with syrup as the end product).

You can sample Québécois wines on the Route des Vins Brome-Missiquoi (www.laroutedesvins.ca), which snakes through the lush vineyards of the region, many of which are notable for their ice wines. Modern wine-making in the region began with the arrival of French-born Christian Barthomeuf in 1977 (now owner of Clos Saragnat), who started producing wine in the 1980s and pioneered the creation of "ice cider" (*cidre de glace*).

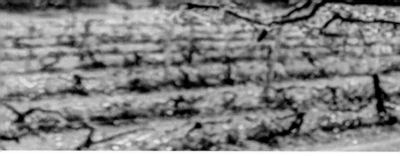

Vineyard welcome sign

DAY 1: BEDFORD

This tour really gets going 75km south-west from Montréal at the small town of **Bedford ①** on the Pike River (Rivière aux Brochets). The main drag, Rue Principale is lined with indie shops and restaurants – be sure to stop at **Capeline & Chocolat** (48 rue Principale; www.facebook.com/capelineetchocolat) to load up with sweet treats. Check out also **Fromagerie Missiska** (100 rue Wheeler; www.missiska. com; Mon and Sun 10am–4pm; Tue 10am–4.30pm; Wed and Thu 10am–5pm; Fri 10am–6pm; Sat 9am–5pm), which sells fine local cheese.

STANBRIDGE EAST

Next, drive 6km east along Rte-202 to **Stanbridge East ②**, where the fas-cinating Moulin Cornell section of the **Musée Missisquoi** (2 rue River; Tue–Sun 11am–4pm; $10; https://musee missisquoi.ca) sheds light on an old grist mill and the 19th-century Fenian Raids. Afterwards stop by **Boulangerie du Capitaine Levain** (5 rue Maple; www. capitainelevain.ca) for freshly baked baguettes, breads, tarts and muffins.

DOMAINE DU RIDGE

Aim to have lunch at your first winery, **Domaine du Ridge ③** (205 chemin Ridge, Saint-Armand; https://domaine duridge.com; May–Oct daily 10am–6pm), 6km south of Stanbridge East. Founded in 1996, this beautifully rustic vineyard produces a particularly good port, as well as Seyval blanc and Vidal blanc whites, and Maréchal Foch and

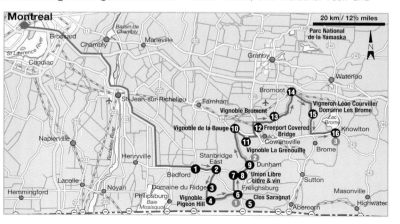

Running in a lavender farm

blended reds. Basic tastings are $15, but you can opt to have charcuterie plates with the wine ($25–35).

VIGNOBLE PIGEON HILL

From Domaine de Ridge it's just 5km further south to the certified organic **Vignoble Pigeon Hill ❹** (395 chemin des Érables, Saint-Armand; https:// vignoblepigeonhill.com; Sat–Sun 11am–5pm). It specializes in wines made with Frontenac noir and Frontenac gris grapes, as well as the Marquette, a hardy Pinot Noir.

FRELIGHSBURG

If Vignoble Pigeon Hill is closed head to similarly organic **Clos Saragnat ❺** (100 chemin de Richford; www.saragnat.com; May to mid-Oct daily 11am–5pm, closed Tue in Sept and Oct; tastings $1–5), 4km southeast from Frelighsburg, homebase of wine and ice cider pioneer Christian Barthomeuf. Tastings take place in the chapel-like stone and stucco boutique. Barthomeuf also runs the adjacent **Domaine Pinnacle** cidery (https:// cidredomainepinnacle.com). Stay the night back in **Frelighsburg ❻** at **Gîte Au Chant de l'Onde** (see page 108); **Restaurant Lyvano** (see ❶) is the best place for dinner. Before leaving town, though, be sure to visit **Les Sucreries De L'Erable** (16 rue Principale; www.les-sucreriesdelerable.com) to sample their celebrated maple syrup pie.

DAY 2: VIGNOBLE DE L'ORPAILLEUR

Make the 7km drive north from Frelighsburg to **Vignoble de l'Orpailleur ❼** (1086 rue Bruce, Dunham; https:// orpailleur.ca; June–Oct daily 10am–5pm; tastings $10) on Rte-202. As well as sampling the wines here, there's an interpretive trail through the vineyard, and there are also guided tours of the winery ($10; reservations required for English guide).

UNION LIBRE CIDRE & VIN AND DUNHAM

Conveniently located 300m down the road from L'Orpailleur, **Union Libre Cidre & Vin ❽** (1047 rue Bruce, Dunham; www.unionlibre.com; check website for latest opening times) produces Vidal, Seyval Blanc and Seyval Noir wines, but also sparkling cider, ice cider and, uniquely, fire cider, made from heated fermented apples. It's just 5km from here into the village of **Dunham ❾**, where **L'Épicerie-Café Dunham** (see ❷) is a good choice for lunch.

VIGNOBLE DE LA BAUGE

Cutting across country, it's 13km from Dunham to **Vignoble de la Bauge ❿** (155 av des Érables, Brigham; https:// labauge.com; tastings $10–12), established by the Naud family in 1986 and

Missisquoi Museum   *Canada's blue grapes*

known today as much for its exotic animal park as its fruity wines and liqueurs.

VIGNOBLE LA GRENOUILLE

It's just 8km to **Vignoble La Grenouille** ⓫ (434 chemin Plouffe, Cowansville; www.vignoblelagrenouille.com; Fri–Sun noon–4pm, check website for full hours), a highly-rated winery just outside of Cowansville. Wines here are named after the word "frog" (*grenouille*) in different languages – the Ixoxo (Zulu for frog) is a highly sought-after red (Marechal Foch). From here it's 10km to **Vignoble Bromont** ⓭ (1095 chemin Nord, Brigham; https://vignoblebromont.ca; tastings $4–12) where you can actually spend the night (see page 108), but make a quick detour to see the charming **Freeport Covered Bridge** ⓬ on route. Crossing an arm of the Yamaska River, the scarlet-painted bridge dates back to 1870.

DAY 3: BROMONT

Start your final day with a 11km drive north along Rte-241, into **Bromont** ⓮, another charming small town best known for the ski resort (www.bromontmontagne.com) that looms over it to the southeast. The main drag, rue Shefford (Rte-241), is lined with pretty wooden homes, shops and restaurants, as well as an impressive church, **Église St-François-Xavier**. The real treat here however is the **Musée du Chocolat** (679 rue Shefford; www.lemu-seeduchocolatdelaconfiseriebromont.com; daily 9am–5pm).

VIGNERON LÉON COURVILLE/ DOMAINE LES BROME

Hit your first winery of the day some 9.5km southeast from Bromont, where **Vigneron Léon Courville/Domaine Les Brome** ⓯ (285 chemin Brome, Ville de Lac-Brome; www.leoncourville.com; Mon–Fri 10am–4pm, Sat–Sun 10am–5pm; tours at 2pm $10) features a superb array of wines – and a gorgeous view of vineyards with Lac Brome shimmering in the distance.

KNOWLTON

Petite **Knowlton** ⓰ on Lac Broome is a short 11km drive from Léon Courville, with **Marina Knowlton** (see ❸) overlooking the lake itself; it's a scenic lunch spot if weather permits. Knowlton's main draw is the chance to spend the afternoon just milling about, sipping coffee and perusing antique shops and art galleries, which you'll find on the two main thoroughfares, chemins Lakeside and Knowlton and other smaller streets.

Boutique Canards Du Lac Brome

Be sure to visit **Boutique Canards Du Lac Brome** (40 chemin du Centre; https://canardsdulacbrome.com; daily 10am–5pm) on the edge of Knowlton, which specializes in duck products. Founded in 1912, it's the oldest company

Knowlton Brome County Museum

producing Pekin ducks in Canada. Among the various lively festivals held throughout the year here is the late-September **Lac Brome Duck Festival**, with culinary demonstrations, a fragrant produce market and plenty of local libations.

Food and Drink

❶ RESTAURANT LYVANO

4 rue Principale, Frelighsburg; tel: 450-298 1119; www.restaurantlyvano.com; Thu–Sun 5–9pm; $$$

Upscale French/Québécois restaurant, serving local produce like maple and herb-glazed duck breast from Lac Brome, and excellent seafood, from pan-seared scallops, cured tuna and poached shrimps, to fish and chips.

❷ L'ÉPICERIE-CAFÉ DUNHAM

3650 rue Principale, Dunham; tel: 450-295 2323; www.lepiceriecafedunham.ca; Wed–Fri 7am–2pm, Sat–Sun 8am–2pm; $$

Attractive café-bistro, serving everything from fluffy omelettes, salads, sandwiches and burgers (with vegetarian and gluten-free options) plus wines and spirits from the Brome-Missisquoi region.

❸ MARINA KNOWLTON

78 rue Benoit, Knowlton; tel: 450-243 545; www.marinaknowlton.com; daily 8am–10pm; $

The main draw at this no-frills bistro is the location, set right on Lac Brome by a small marina, with outdoor tables on the deck. Serves simple food – burgers, salads and the like – and perfect for sunset drinks.

Société Historique du Comté du Brome

The **Brome County Museum** (130 chemin Lakeside; www.bromemuseum.com; mid-May to Oct daily 10am–5pm, Sun 11am–4.30pm; Nov to mid-May Mon–Sat 10am–4pm; $8) complex features the 19th-century **Paul Holland Knowlton House** crammed with regional cultural artefacts, many of which reveal the Loyalist history of the province. The **Martin Annex** holds a number of military pieces, including a World War I Fokker DVII airplane. There's also the **Old Fire Hall**, containing a general store, blacksmith's shop, post office, and vintage radio display. The original **Knowlton Academy** building of 1854 houses a schoolroom and an exhibit about the thousands of British children who passed through here at the end of the 19th century. The historical society also runs the **Children's Museum** in the Marion Phelps Building, which invites the younger set to step back into the past, with an array of interactive exhibits and more.

Theatre Lac Brome

The **Theatre Lac Brome** (9 chemin Mont-Écho; https://theatrelacbrome.ca) showcases English-language plays, and live music, from folk to classical. End your trip with a show here, before the 1hr 30min drive back to Montréal (105km).

Biking Eastern Townships

PEDALLING THE CANTONS DE L'EST: GRANDES FOURCHES

Rolling hills punctuated by parish churches and quiet rivers winding through the countryside: the Cantons-de-l'Est are ideal for exploring on two wheels. This loop from Sherbrooke takes in berry farms, mountain lakes and microbreweries.

DISTANCE: 52km
TIME: 2 Days
START/END: Marché de la Gare de Sherbrooke
POINTS TO NOTE: This tour is designed as a bike trip – you can rent bicycles in Sherbrooke (near the starting point of this route) at Café-Vélo des Nations (9 rue de la Glacière; www.cafevelodesnations. com; $25/day, $60/day for electric bike). You can buy maps or get them online at www.routeverte.com, though signposts make it hard to get lost. The route assumes spring, summer and fall travel – although many sights on the route close from September to May, the roads themselves are usually open year-round and much of the region comes alive with winter sports and activities at that time. The main tourist information centres on route are the Sherbrooke Tourist Office (785 rue King Ouest; http://destination sherbrooke.com), and the North Hatley Tourist Office (300 rue Mill; www.north hatley.org). For accommodation options see page 108.

In addition to its vineyards, sugar shacks and ski resorts, the Cantons-de-l'Est are prime cycling territory. This route follows the Grandes Fourches Circuit, covering the highlights on a loop from Sherbrooke. It's just a taster, however – the trail follows just a tiny segment of the Route Verte (Green Route; www.routeverte. com) network that smothers Québec like a giant web. With over 5,300km of trails, it's the biggest network of bicycle trails in North America. The Grandes Fourches Circuit takes in some of the most enticing, primarily wooded country of the Cantons-de-l'Est, with 22km of unpaved bike path, 10km of paved bike path and the rest on minor roads.

MARCHÉ DE LA GARE DE SHERBROOKE

Start the day at the local market, the **Marché de la Gare de Sherbrooke ❶** (710 place de la Gare; https://marchede lagare.com; Sat–Wed 9am–6pm, Thu–Fri 9am–8pm), a great spot for breakfast and for picnic supplies – it's stocked with sellers of local produce (see ❶).

Hydro electric dam on Magog River in Sherbrooke

THE MAGOG RIVER VALLEY

From the market cross the **Magog River** on the dedicated pedestrian/cycle bridge and follow the paved bike trail west, along the northern shore of the river, known here as the "**Lac du Nations**" ❷. The route keeps to the north bank of the river, though the dedicated bike path eventually ends and the route runs along Rue Mills. After around 11km you'll cross the Magog again on **Chemin Saint-Roch** ❸ in Rock Forest – the route merges here with the signposted Route Verte 1, which you will now follow all the way back to Sherbrooke. It briefly runs east then due south, cutting through **Base de Plein Air André-Nadeau** ❹, a park that offers year-round activities. The trail leads south for 10km, eventually onto Chemin Beaudette and Chemin de l'Université – both quiet roads with very light

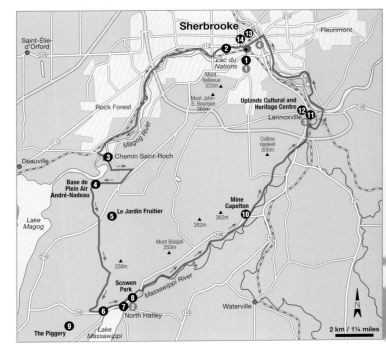

One of many bike signs

Memphremagog Lake in Magog

traffic – before cutting down into **North Hatley** on Rte-108.

Le Jardin Fruitier

It's worth making a short detour on route to North Hatley to visit **Le Jardin Fruitier ❺** (www.jardinfruitier.com; daily 8am–6pm), some 850m east of the trail on Rue de Lotbinière. It's a rustic berry farm where in season you can pick fresh strawberries, raspberries, blueberries and blackberries.

NORTH HATLEY AND LAKE MASSAWIPPI

It's here that the unique flavour of the Magog region really come together. **Lake Massawippi ❻** offers some of the most idyllic waterfront spots in the region, with a couple of splendid lakeside inns – it's worth spending the night here (see page 108), though veteran cyclists will be able to complete the loop in one day. The tiny town of **North Hatley ❼**, which sits at the northern tip of the lake, charmingly reveals its anglophone roots, with boutiques selling teas and tweeds. Be sure to sample the food and the pastries at **Saveurs Et Gourmandises** (see ❷) on the banks of the lake, and the local souvenirs and chocolates at **Auberge la Chocolatiere** (312 chemin de la Rivière; www.aubergela-chocolatiere.com). For an easy hike, stroll the wooded trails of **Scowen Park ❽** on the north side of the village. You can also take a cruise on the lake on

"Le Wippi", which shuttles between North Hatley and Ayer's Cliff six times daily (late June to early Sept). On Saturdays there's a farmers' market along the river in the **Parc de la Rivière**.

Around 3km west of the village is **The Piggery ❾** (215 chemin Simard; www.piggery.com), which puts on an eclectic array of shows, from musicals to bluegrass, throughout the summer – try and book tickets in advance. **Parc Dreamland**, overlooking the lake in the heart of the village, hosts free outdoor concerts on Saturday and Sunday evenings through July and August.

MASSAWIPPI RIVER VALLEY

Beyond North Hatley the route cuts northeast along the beautifully wooded **Massawippi River Valley**, mostly on blissfully traffic-free unpaved bike trail. It's relatively flat so you'll have plenty of time to explore sights along the way.

Mine Capelton

Some 9km north of North Hatley, where the bike path crosses underneath Rte-108, **Mine Capelton ❿** (5800 chemin Capelton; www.capelton.ca; $41.20) makes for a fascinating pit-stop. This old copper mine dates back to 1863, and today guides take you underground to tour some of the old workings – you can also pan for gold in the nearby stream. Your ticket includes the truck ride up and down Mont Capel to the mine entrance.

LENNOXVILLE

From the mine it's about 7km to the small town of **Lennoxville** ⓫, where the Massawippi flows into the Saint-François River. The bike trail runs through Bishop's University campus and crosses the Saint-François River on St Francis Street, but it's worth making a detour into the downtown area, on the other side of the Massawippi. Have lunch at **Le Lion d'Or** (see ❸), notable as the first microbrewery to open in Québec, back in 1986.

Uplands Cultural and Heritage Centre
The **Uplands Cultural and Heritage Centre** ⓬ (9 rue Speid; http://uplands. ca; see website for hours) in Lennoxville exhibits the work of local and regional artists, and displays a large collection of local antiques. Traditional English tea (with scones) is also served on the veranda. The property itself is a Georgian-style gem constructed in 1862 for English settler John Paddon – the house was purchased by the town in 1987.

SAINT-FRANÇOIS RIVER VALLEY

The final leg of the route runs some 5km along the north bank of the Saint-François River into Sherbrooke, on a mixture of paved and unpaved bike path. Sherbrooke has its origins in a settlement founded by American Loyalist Gilbert Hyatt in 1793, known as "Hyatt's Mills". It was renamed after Governor General Sir John Sherbrooke in 1818

and flourished as a manufacturing centre. Today the Université de Sherbrooke is the biggest employer.

SHERBROOKE

Linger in the university town of **Sherbrooke** ⓭, which has a youthful energy and is evolving from a gritty commercial hub to a lively city with some worthwhile sights and innovative restaurants. Most of the city's attractions are clustered in **Vieux-Sherbrooke**, around the 1.5km gorge carved by the Magog River. The city also boasts several microbreweries that serve food; try **Siboire Dépôt** (see ❹).

Musée des Beaux Arts de Sherbrooke
The absorbing **Musée des Beaux Arts de Sherbrooke** (241 rue Dufferin; http:// mbas.qc.ca; Wed–Sun 10.30am–4pm; $10), housed in a handsome 19th-century building, displays a range of works by Québécois artists, from the 19th century to today, including Frederick Simpson Coburn, Charles Daudelin and Michel Goulet. The museum also features interesting temporary exhibits, often with a focus on local art and sculpture.

Musée d'Histoire de Sherbrooke
Next door to the art museum, the **Musée d'Histoire de Sherbrooke** (275 rue Dufferin; https://mhist.org; Wed–Fri 10am–noon and 1–4.30pm, Sat–Sun noon–4.30pm; $10) delves into the history of Sherbrooke, from permanent exhibits on the evolution of urban sprawl

Part of the century Story of Sherbrooke Fresco Murals

to temporary shows that showcase topics like the musical history of the city.

Musée de la Nature et des Sciences de Sherbrooke

Overlooking the Magog River gorge on the south side, the **Musée de la Nature et des Sciences de Sherbrooke** (225 rue Frontenac; https://mns2.ca; late June to early Sept Wed–Sun 9am–4.30; see website for seasonal hours; $13) highlights popular science and environmental issues with interactive rotating exhibits, plus permanent collections of rocks and minerals, and vast numbers of bird, mammal and fossil specimens from Québec.

Promenade de la Gorge de la Magog

Finally, before leaving Sherbrooke, take some time to wander the walkway along the gorgeous **Magog River Gorge** ⑭ itself, which runs along the bank of the river for half a kilometre or so in the centre of town, from the Porte de la Gorge (Rue Richmond) to Porte des Fabriques (Rue Frontenac).

Food and Drink

① MARCHÉ DE LA GARE DE SHERBROOKE

710 place de la Gare, Sherbrooke; tel: 819-569 0909; https://marchedela gare.ca; Sat–Wed 9am–6pm, Thu–Fri 9am–8pm; $
Sherbrooke's public market is a great place to stock up on local food and drink products, with stalls selling Quartier oriental kebabs, cheese from Fromages du P'tit Mont Ham and cider from Cidrerie de Compton.

② SAVEURS ET GOURMANDISES

39 rue Main, North Hatley; tel: 819-842 3131; Tue–Sun 9am–4pm; $
Fabulous café and bakery that sells wonderfully fresh breads, croissants and viennoiseries, but also quiches, soups, salads, pizza and smoked salmon.

③ LE LION D'OR

2902 College St, Lennoxville; tel: 819-565 1015; www.lionlennoxville.com; Tue–Sat 3–11pm; $
The Golden Lion pioneered Québec's craft beer scene in the 1980s, with its blueberry wheat, pale ale, bitter and Lion's Pride ales just as good as always. The food is pretty good too; hearty steaks, ribs and poutines, with live entertainment most evenings and lots of live hockey on TV.

④ SIBOIRE DÉPÔT

80 rue du Dépôt, Sherbrooke; tel: 819-565 3636; https://siboire.ca; daily 11.30am–9pm; $$
This outpost of the local craft brewery is housed in the old station, spacious, atmospheric digs in which to sample its locally celebrated fish and chips (haddock, salmon or cod), and range of beers, from its session IPAs to oatmeal stout.

THE CENTRE: MONTRÉAL TO QUÉBEC CITY

This route traverses the culturally rich heart of Québec, along the St Lawrence River Valley between Montréal and Québec City – taking in historic French villages, old windmills, spectacular river views and the enchanting old city of Trois-Rivières.

DISTANCE: 360km

TIME: 3 days

START: Montréal

END: Québec City

POINTS TO NOTE: This tour is designed as a road-trip. At its southern end the route can be extended with the walking tours around Montréal (see pages 26 and 32) and the road trips through the wine region (see page 44) and Laurentians (see page 38). At its northern end it links to the l'Île-d'Orléans Loop (see page 68), the Beaupré/ Charlevoix route (see page 73) and the Bas-Saint-Laurent route (see page 92). The route has been primarily designed for spring, summer and fall travel – although many sights on the route close completely or partially from September to May, the roads are usually open year-round and much of the region comes alive with winter sports and activities at that time. Some sights are usually closed on Mondays and Tuesdays (year round). For accommodation options on the route see page 108.

This route cuts through the heart of Québec, following the old Chemin du Roy ("King's Road") along the north bank of the St Lawrence to Trois-Riv-ières, then switching to the south to traverse the Route des Navigateurs to Québec City. Chief Surveyor Jean-Eu-stache Lanouiller de Boisclerc began work on Le Chemin du Roy back in 1731, at the behest of the French colo-nial authorities – it ran 280km, was made of crushed piles of rocks, and took six years to complete. Thereafter the road served horse couriers, car-riages, stagecoaches, mail coaches and, during winter, sleighs. Today, Rte-138 traces much of the old route, through the regions of Lanaudière and Mauricie. The Route des Navigateurs follows the southern bank of the St Lawrence via Rte-132, slicing through the regions of Centre-du-Québec and Chaudière-Appalaches, and is marked with easily recognizable blue signs. For information on the Centre-du-Québec region, visit www.tourisme centreduquebec.com; for Lanaudière visit https://lanaudiere.ca; for Mau-

Maple taffy

icie www.mauricietourism.com; and or Chaudière-Appalaches https:// chaudiereappalaches.com.

DAY 1: THE NORTH SHORE: LE CHEMIN DU ROY

Start your journey in the suburban riverside town of **Repentigny ❶**, 37km north of Downtown Montréal. Founded in 1670, it was traditionally the southwestern terminus of the **King's Road**. Grab breakfast in **Brûlerie du Roy** (see ❶), opposite the art centre in the heart of town. Repentigny marks the start of the generally rural **Lanaudière** region of Québec that runs along the north shore of the St Lawrence – it was named in 1960 after Charlotte de Lanaudière, the wife of pioneer Barthélemy Joliette, both of whom were from important *seigneur* families. Lanaudière is also known as a cradle of Québec music: many of the best-loved folk music groups and singers in the province hail from here, including national treasure **Céline Dion**, who grew up in Charlemagne, a few kilometres southwest of Repentigny.

Centre d'art Diane-Dufresne

The stylish **Centre d'art Diane-Dufresne** (11 Allée de la Création; https:// espaceculturel.repentigny.ca/fr/ centre-art-diane-dufresne; Wed–Fri 1– 5pm, Sat–Sun 10am–5pm; check website for latest hours; $8) in Repentigny showcases visual art and local arts and

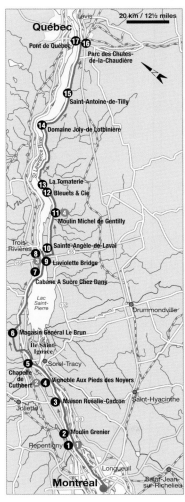

Variatons of maple syru,

crafts through mostly travelling exhibitions. The glinting stainless steel building is part of the attraction, designed by Montréal-based ACDF Architecture in 2015 and set in wonderfully landscaped grounds. On your way out of Repentigny on Rte-138, stop for a quick look at the **Moulin Grenier ❷**, a fairytale windmill built in 1820.

Maison Rosalie-Cadron

Some 23km north from Repentigny on Rte-138, it's worth stopping at the tiny **Maison Rosalie-Cadron ❸** (1997 rue Notre-Dame, Lavaltrie; http://maison-rosaliecadron.org; late June to early Sept Wed–Sun 10am–5pm; $7), a modest, all-white clapboard house built in 1790. It was the birthplace of **Rosalie Cadron-Jetté** in 1794, who went on to found the Sisters of Mercy in 1848, a Catholic charitable organization dedicated to helping unwed mothers and their children. The house has been restored to its circa 1822 appearance, with costumed guides adding colour.

Vignoble Aux Pieds des Noyers

From Maison Rosalie-Cadron it's just 9km along Rte-138 to **Vignoble Aux Pieds des Noyers ❹** (71 Grande-Côte, Lanoraie; www.auxpiedsdesnoyers. com); reserve in advance where possible. This is a winery where you can also get lunch (alternatively **Casse Croute Chez Cocotte**, see ❼, is a bit further along the road).

Lanaudière has a growing reputation as a wine-producing region, and this was the pioneer, with a decent range o reds and whites being produced toda (mainly white Gewürztraminer ano Chardonnay).

Chapelle de Cuthbert

The small town of **Berthierville** lies 15km along Rte-138 from Aux Pieds des Noyers, home to oldest former Protestant church in Québec. The modes **Chapelle de Cuthbert ❺** (461 rue de Bienville; www.chapelledescuthbert com; June–Sept Wed–Sun 9am–6pm was built in 1786 by Scottish-bornn James Cuthbert (it was originally a Presbyterian chapel dedicated to St Andrew).

Though it's historically significant there's not much to see inside – it now serves as a small gallery with occasional exhibitions.

Magasin Général Le Brun

It's another 20km to the charming **Magasin Général Le Brun ❻** (192 Route du Pied de la Côte; https:// magasingenerallebrun.com; daily 10am–5pm), located off Rte-138 in the tiny village of **Lebrun**.

This old general store sells just about everything, including plenty o local souvenirs and products. It dates back to 1915, but there have been trading posts on this site since 1803.

You've now left the Lanaudière region and are travelling across **Mauricie** named after the Saint-Maurice River.

Manoir Boucher–De Niverville

Cabane A Sucre Chez Dany

If you can, stop at **Cabane A Sucre Chez Dany** ❼ (195 rue de la Sablière; http://cabanechezdany.com), a beloved sugar shack 37km from Lebrun in **Village-des-Crête**, just outside Trois-Rivières. This is the spot to try maple syrup on snow, maple taffy and buy all sorts of maple products. It also serves hearty meals for dinner. It's just 11km into central **Trois-Rivières** from here – for accommodation, see page 108.

DAY 2: TROIS-RIVIÈRES

Devote the whole of day two to **Trois-Rivières** ❽, the lively hub of the Mauricie region. The town sits at the point where the Rivière St-Maurice splits into three channels – hence the name "Three Rivers" – before meeting the St Lawrence. The European settlement dates from 1634, when it established itself as an embarkation point for the French explorers of the continent and as an iron-ore centre. Lumber followed, and today Trois-Rivières is one of the largest producers of paper in the world. Today the city's compact downtown core branches off from the small square of **Parc Champlain** and extends south down to the waterfront, its shady streets lined with historic buildings. This day-tour can be completed on foot (just over 2km one-way), but you might want to drive or get a taxi to and from Borealis.

Cathédrale de l'Assomption

Dominating the north side of Parc Champlain is stately **Cathédrale de l'Assomption**, primarily notable for its 125 sensational stained-glass windows by Guido Nincheri, and its distinctive Gothic Revival style. This church was inaugurated in 1858, but there's been a place of worship here since the late 17th century.

Manoir Boucher de Niverville

From the cathedral it's a short walk along Rue Bonaventure, lined with some of the prettiest historic houses in the city, to the white stone **Manoir Boucher de Niverville** (168 rue Bonaventure; www.cultur3r.com/lieux/manoir-boucher-de-niverville; late June to early Sept daily 10am–6pm; $4), a manor house built in 1668. Exhibitions inside shed light on middle-class life in colonial Québec. The house is named after Joseph-Claude Boucher de Niverville, local *seigneur*, who inherited it in 1761.

Musée POP-La Culture Populaire du Québec

From the Manoir retrace your steps back up Bonaventure and turn right (north) on Rue Heel; a couple of blocks away is the modern **Musée POP-La Culture Populaire du Québec** (200 rue Laviolette; https://musee-pop.ca; late June to early Sept daily 10am–5pm; see website for seasonal hours; museum $15, jail $17; com-

Laviolette Bridge

bined $24). The museum features folk and pop culture exhibitions, including everything from local crafts to an overview of sports stars of the province. The real highlight is the **Vielle Prison of Trois-Rivières**, which operated from 1822 to 1986.

While the decades of graffiti tell a story, it's nothing compared to the tales of the guides – some of them once served time here. You can only visit the prison on guided tours (1hr 30min); as your ticket is valid for the entire day, have lunch nearby at **La P'tite Brûlerie** (see ❸).

St. James Church and Musée des Ursulines

In the afternoon, walk south down Rue Saint François Xavier, past more historic homes, and take a peek at **St. James Church** (late June to early Sept daily 10am–6pm) on the corner of Rue des Ursulines. It was built by French Récollets missionaries in 1754, but was abandoned and became an Anglican church in 1823.

This section of Rue des Ursulines is the oldest district of Trois-Rivières, and looks it. The **Musée des Ursulines** (734 rue des Ursulines; www.musee-ursulines.qc.ca; late June to early Sept daily 10am–5pm; see website for seasonal hours; $7) occupies the old Ursuline nunnery and showcases its fascinating history as a religious house, school and hospital since the 17th century.

Musée Boréalis

End your tour of Trois-Rivières with a look at its more recent history. The **Musée Boréalis** (200 av des Draveurs; www.borealis3r.ca; late June to early Sept daily 10am–6pm; $11) occupies the former filtration plant of the Canadian International Paper factory, overlooking the Saint-Maurice and S Lawrence rivers – it lies around 1km from the Ursuline nunnery. The interactive, multimedia exhibits here showcase the history of the pulp and paper industry that has had such a huge impact on Trois-Rivières.

Cirque du Soleil

Try to snag tickets to the summer performances (July–Aug) held in Trois-Rivières by **Cirque du Soleil** (www.cirquedusoleil.com). As it's such a popular thing to do – not just here but around the world – it's best to book tickets in advance, if possible. The world-famous company agreed to hold specially created shows at the outdoor **Amphithéâtre Cogeco** (100 av des Draveurs; www.amphitheatrecogeco.com), next to Borealis, until at least 2024.

DAY 3: THE SOUTH SHORE - ROUTE DES NAVIGATEURS

Start the last day of the tour by crossing the huge 2.7km **Laviolette Bridge** ❾ across the St Lawrence onto the south shore, where the **Route des Navigateurs** (Rte-132) continues

Ursuline Convent

Domaine Joly–De Lotbinière

northeast towards Québec City. This is now the heavily agricultural **Centre-du-Québec** region.

Sainte-Angèle-de-Laval

Drive 19km from central Trois-Rivières to the small riverside community of **Sainte-Angèle-de-Laval ⑩**, where the **Centre de la Biodiversité du Québec** (1800 av des Jasmins; www.biodiversite.net; daily 10am–4pm; $12) does a good job of showcasing the flora and fauna of Québec, with "Sushi" the river otter and "Bibi" the white-tailed deer star attractions (the facilities are well-managed and inspected regularly). A little further in the heart of the village, the **La Maison de Bibi** (14840 blvd Bécancour; www.lamaisondebibi.com; Mon–Sat 8.30am–5.30pm, Sun 8.30pm–5pm) specialises in local artisanal soap, but also sells fudge, jams and desserts (there's also a café here). The village is also known for its excellent microbrewery, **Ô Quai des Brasseurs** (https://oquaidesbrasseurs.com; Sun–Wed 11am–11pm, Thu–Fri 11am–1am), where you can pick up some beers to go.

Moulin Michel de Gentilly

The **Moulin Michel de Gentilly ⑪** (www.moulinmichel.qc.ca; late June to early Sept daily 10am–5pm; $8), a beautifully sited historic flourmill, is around 25km from Sainte-Angèle on Rte-132. The mill dates back to 1783, and was used to process buckwheat flour commercially right up to 1972. Costumed guides give guided tours of the hydro-powered mill interior, while exhibits explore the history of the site. Today the old stone wheels have been revived and still grind flour – have lunch here at the **Crêperie Champêtre** (see ④), to taste the finished product.

Bleuets & Cie and La Tomaterie

If you're still interested in sampling the rich natural produce of the region, make a stop at **Bleuets & Cie ⑫** (tel: 819-263 0286), 8.5km north of Moulin Michel on Rte-132, where you can pick your own blueberries (or just buy them). Just 2km further along in Saint-Pierre-les-Becquets, **La Tomaterie ⑬** (https://latomaterie.com; open Easter to Sept, variable hours) is a fabulous local produce market.

Domaine Joly-de Lotbinière

From Saint-Pierre-les-Becquets Rte-132 winds along the banks of the St Lawrence for 37km to the beautiful gardens of the **Domaine Joly-de Lotbinière ⑭** (www.domainejoly.com; $12–20; check the bloom calendar on the website to plan your visit). In addition to 11 different gardens (part English, part French style), developed by the *seigneurs* of Lotbinière since 1908, there are woodland trails, beaches, and a gorgeous manor, the Maple House, built by Henri-Gustave Joly de Lotbinière as a summer residence in 1851.

Chaudière River Fa...

You're now in the **Chaudière-Appalaches** region south of Québec City, encompassing most of the traditional **Beauce**, the fiercely independent, entrepreneurial heartland of the province.

Parc des Chutes-de-la-Chaudière

From the gardens, Rte-132 continues to shadow the St Lawrence, passing through several pretty villages. One that's particularly worth visiting is **Saint-Antoine-de-Tilly** ⓯. Continue on all the way to Québec City. If there's time it's also worth stopping at the **Parc de Chutes-de-la-Chaudière** ⓰ (free), som 50km from Domaine Joly-de Lotbinièr Embrace the fresh air and stretch you legs with a short stroll. These 35-metr tall waterfalls on the Chaudière Rive are pretty impressive, especially whe viewed from the waterside trails and sus pension bridge downstream.

From here it's a short drive over th famous **Pont de Québec** ⓱ into the cit – the longest cantilever bridge in th world.

Food and Drink

❶ BRÛLERIE DU ROY

440 rue Notre-Dame, Repentigny; tel: 450-932 6652; www.brulerieduroy.com; Tue–Fri 8am–5pm, Sat 9am–5pm, Sun 10am–5pm; $
This branch of the Lanaudière mini coffee shop chain has a warm, contemporary style, with exceptional espresso coffees, excellent croissants and a variety of light breakfasts and lunches.

❷ CASSE CROUTE CHEZ COCOTTE

532 Grande Côte Est, Lanoraie; tel: 450-803 2476; Wed–Sun 11am–8pm; $
This roadside shack (a converted bus with outdoor tables) right on the St Lawrence offers surprisingly tasty meals, with sandwiches, poutines, shrimp rolls, cheeseburgers and more.

❸ LA P'TITE BRÛLERIE

363 rue Laviolette, Trois-Rivières; tel: 819-375 6890; Mon–Fri 8am–5pm; $
This café/used books store is a wonderful place for a light meal, cake, croissant and a coffee (with fabulous single origins and blends), surrounded by stacks of books – they do good salads and sandwiches.

❹ CRÊPERIE CHAMPÊTRE

Moulin Michel De Gentilly, 675 blvd Bécancour (Rte-132), Bécancour; tel: 819-298 2882; www.moulinmichel.qc.ca; daily 11am–4pm; $$
The in-house restaurant at the Moulin Michel specialises in crêpes and de *galettes de sarrasin* (buckwheat pancakes), made with flour milled on the premises, enhanced with toppings sourced from local fruit, honey and meat farms. Meals are served on the terrace in fine weather.

Notre-Dame-des-Victoires Church

A WALK AROUND VIEUX-QUÉBEC (OLD QUÉBEC)

This tour explores Old Québec, the only walled city in North America, taking in the cobbled streets of the Quartier du Petit-Champlain, the iconic Château Frontenac, and the ace views from the Terrasse Dufferin, perched above the St Lawrence River.

DISTANCE: 2km

TIME: A full day

START: Place Royale, Basse-Ville

END: Porte St-Jean, Haute-Ville

POINTS TO NOTE: If you're planning to visit any of the museums, avoid doing this walk on a Monday, as some of the sights close on that day – most attractions otherwise open daily in the summer months, but have reduced hours or close completely thereafter. The tour can be easily completed on foot, so if you're looking for a walking option then this could be an ideal route for you to take. Note, though, that there is some up and down (the funicular railway takes care of the first climb up), and it's not suitable (or that interesting) for young children. For accommodation in Québec City see page 108.

Spread over the promontory of Cap Dia-mant and the banks of the St Lawrence River, Québec City is one of the most beautifully located cities in Canada. Vieux-Québec, the old city surrounded by solid fortifications, is a UNESCO World Heritage Site. Throughout, winding cobbled streets are flanked by 17th- and 18th-century stone houses and churches, graceful parks and squares, and countless monuments. Over ninety percent of its 800,000 population are francophone, and it is often difficult to remember which continent you are on as you tuck into a croissant and *café au lait* in a Parisian-style café. None of Québec City's highlights are far from the St Lawrence River, with the main attractions being evenly distributed between the upper (Haut) and lower (Basse) portions of Vieux-Québec. This one-day tour winds its way around the highlights.

PLACE ROYALE

Begin where it all started in 1608, **Place Royale ❶** in Basse-Ville. Champlain built the first permanent base in New France here in order to begin trading fur with the Indigenous peoples. After a long period of disrepair, today its pristine stone houses, most of which date from around 1685, are undeniably photogenic, with

their steep metal roofs, numerous chimneys and pastel-coloured shutters. Happily, the atmosphere is enlivened in summer by entertainment from classi-

cal orchestras to juggling clowns, and by the Fêtes de la Nouvelle-France, where everyone dresses in period costume and it once again becomes a chaotic

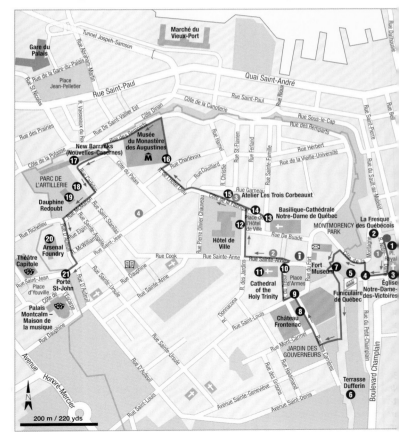

Vieux–Québec view

marketplace. Have breakfast or a quality coffee at **Smith Café** (see ❶), which overlooks the square. Just to the north along Rue Notre Dame, check out the building-sized **La Fresque des Québécois** ❷ (Québéc city mural), a dramatic trompe-l'oeil work unveiled in 1999 telling the story of the city.

Église Notre-Dame-des-Victoires

The **Église Notre-Dame-des-Victoires** ❸ (www.notre-dame-de-quebec.org; mid-May to late June daily 9.30am–5pm; late June to Aug daily 9.30am–6.30pm; Sept–Oct Wed–Sat noon–4pm, Sun 9.30am–4.30pm), on the west side of Place Royale, was established in 1688 and has been completely restored twice – after destruction by shellfire in 1759 and a fire in 1969. Inside, the fortress-shaped altar alludes to the two French victories over the British navy (in 1690 and 1711) that gave the church its name. Paintings depicting these events hang above the altar, while the aisles are lined with copies of religious paintings by Van Dyck, Van Loo and Rubens, gifts from early settlers to give thanks for a safe passage. The large model ship suspended in the nave has a similar origin.

QUARTIER DU PETIT-CHAMPLAIN

Behind the church, walk along Rue Notre-Dame into the **Quartier du Petit-Champlain** – the oldest shopping area in North America. The quaint 17th- and 18th-century houses now hold restaurants, boutiques and galleries selling arts and crafts. Turn right on Rue Sous-Le-Fort; this curves to the south to become narrow, cobbled **Rue du Petit-Champlain** ❹. Dating back to 1685, this is the city's oldest street.

Funiculaire de Québec

When you've finished perusing Rue du Petit-Champlain, head back to the 17th-century **Maison Louis-Jolliet** at No. 16, which houses the base station for the short **Funiculaire de Québec** ❺ (www.funiculaire.ca; daily: Jan–Mar and Dec 7.30am–10.30pm; Apr to late June and Sept–Oct 7.30am–11pm; late June to Aug 7.30am–11.30pm; Nov Mon–Fri 7.30am–9pm, Sat–Sun 10am–7pm; $3.75). First established in 1879, the (now modernized) funicular shoots up the 60-meter high cliff in a couple of minutes, transporting you from Bass-Ville to Haute-Ville in a matter of seconds. If you'd prefer the short but steep hike, walk up the adjacent **L'Escalier Casse-Cou** (Breakneck Stairs) and follow Côte de la Montagne around to the top.

TERRASSE DUFFERIN

The Funiculaire de Québec spits you out at the clifftop boardwalk of the **Terrasse Dufferin** ❻ in front of the Château Frontenac, a spectacular vantage point over Basse-Ville and the St Lawrence. Here is a romantic statue of Champlain and, beside it, a modern sculpture symbolizing Québec City's status as a UNESCO World

Funiculaire

Heritage Site. History buffs may want to buy tickets at the Frontenac Kiosk for **Lieu historique national des Forts-et-Châteaux-Saint-Louis ❼** (www.pc.gc.ca/fr/lhn-nhs/qc/saintlouisforts; mid-May to early Oct daily 9am–6pm; $3.90),

the enigmatic ruins of Château St-Louis underneath the boardwalk. The fortress served as the governor's residence for two centuries until a fire destroyed it in 1834. Today, little remains of it, but the foundations, weathered stone walls and 120 artefacts found on site (including pipes dating back to Champlain's time) are enigmatic enough, enhanced with audio and plenty of information.

CHÂTEAU FRONTENAC

Looming over the Terrasse Dufferin is the iconic **Château Frontenac ❽** (www.fairmont.com/frontenac-quebec), a pseudo-medieval pile crowned with a copper roof. Although the hotel was inaugurated by the Canadian Pacific Railway in 1893, its distinctive main tower was only added in the early 1920s, resulting in an over-the-top design that makes the most of the stupendous location atop Cap Diamant. Numerous notables, including Queen Elizabeth II, have stayed here, and suites have been named after Churchill and Roosevelt who were holed up in the hotel during the First and Second Quebec Conferences of World War II.

A small exhibit charts the history of the hotel in the ornate lobby, but you can also take a guided tour (daily; visit www.cicerone.ca/en/guided-tours for the latest schedule; guided tours $21, $15 for guests), or connect to the hotel wi-fi (free to the public) and download the virtual tour app.

Place Royale   *Frontenac castle*

PLACE D'ARMES

The north side of Château Frontenac faces Haute-Ville's main square, the **Place d'Armes** , with benches around the central fountain. Champlain established his first fort here in 1620, on the site now occupied by the hotel. On the west side of the square is the former Palais de Justice, a Renaissance-style courthouse completed in 1887 to a design by Eugène-Étienne Taché, architect of the province's Parliament buildings (it's now a Ministry of Finance building).

Rue du Trésor and Les Artisans de la Cathédrale

Leading off the northwest corner of Place d'Armes is the narrow alley of **Rue du Trésor** , where French settlers once paid their taxes to the Royal Treasury; nowadays it's a local artists' market. There's also a row of stalls and portraitists on the pedestrianized stretch of **Rue Ste-Anne**, which runs west off Trésor, and in the churchyard running alongside it, "**Les Artisans de la Cathédrale**". Grab a typical French/ Québécois lunch at **Chez Jules** (see), at 24 Rue Ste-Anne.

CATHEDRAL OF THE HOLY TRINITY

"Les Artisans de la Cathédrale" stalls lie inside the grounds of the **Cathedral of the Holy Trinity** (www.cathedral. ca; late May to Oct daily 10am–5pm), whose main entrance lies at the western end of Rue Ste-Anne on Rue des Jardins.

This was the first Anglican cathedral built outside the British Isles. Constructed between 1800 and 1804, it followed the lines of the church of St Martin-in-the-Fields in London. Many of the church's features came from London, including lavish silverware from George III (displayed in the special "King's Gift" exhibit along with rare Bibles; $2 donation requested) and Victorian stained glass, shipped in vats of molasses for protection.

PLACE DE L'HÔTEL DE VILLE

From the cathedral stroll one block north along Rue des Jardins to the civic heart of Haute-Ville, the **Place de l'Hôtel de Ville** . Dominated by the Monument Cardinal-Taschereau in the centre, it's the scene of numerous live shows in summer. Facing each other on opposite sides of the square lie the edifices of the colony's once-powerful Church and the home of democratic power in the city today – the **Hôtel de Ville (City Hall)** of 1883.

Basilique-Cathédrale Notre-Dame de Québec

The eastern side of Place de l'Hôtel de Ville is dominated by the impressive bulk of the **Basilique-Cathédrale Notre-Dame de Québec** (www.notre-dame-de-quebec.org; Mon–Fri 7am–4pm, Sat 7am–6pm, Sun 8am–5pm), the oldest parish north of Mexico. The church burnt to the ground in 1922 and was rebuilt to the original plans of its 17th-century

Monument to Samuel De Champlain, founder of the Québec City at the Place D'Arme

forebear; the Rococo-inspired interior culminates in a ceiling of blue sky and billowy clouds. On the right side of the basilica lies the tomb of **Saint François de Laval**, one of the founding fathers of Québec. Visit the **Centre d'Animation François-de Laval** (http://francois-delaval.com; daily 9am–5pm; free) in the chapel beyond the tomb to learn more about Laval.

Côte de la Fabrique

From the northwest corner of Place de l'Hôtel de Ville, wander down **Côte de la Fabrique ⑭**, lined with interesting indie shops and cafés. Grab a coffee and snack at **Baguette & Chocolat** (see ❶) at No. 36, before checking out **Atelier Les Trois Corbeaux ⑮** (Three Crow Glass Studio) at No. 41 (https://troiscorbeaux.com; daily 10am–6pm), best known for its demonstrations of traditional glass-blowing.

MUSÉE DU MONASTÈRE DES AUGUSTINES

At the bottom of Côte de la Fabrique, look for narrow Rue de l'Hôtel Dieu on the right (leading northwest) and walk to the end – you should see the back entrance to the fascinating **Musée du Monastère des Augustines ⑯** (https://monastere.ca/en/pages/museum; Tue–Sun 10am–5pm; $11.50), a little to the right on Rue Charlevoix. Québec's old Augustinian convent has been tastefully converted into a boutique hotel and an intriguing museum. The museum tells the story of the Augustinian Sisters, who came to Québec in 1639 primarily to nurse the sick. Objects displayed include scary looking surgical instruments from the 18th century.

NEW BARRACKS

End your tour with a look at the famous walls and fortifications of the city. Leave the Augustinian convent by the front entrance and you'll be on **Rue des Remparts**, with a wonderful view down to Basse-Ville and Saint-Roch business district. Turn left (west) and walk down to the junction with Côte du Palais, where you'll see the **New Barracks (Nouvelles Casernes) ⑰**, built by the French between 1749 and 1752 and later serving as a barracks for the Royal Artillery Regiment. The ambitious renovation of this building is likely to be complete sometime in 2022. Get a closer look by walking west along Rue de l'Arsenal. Keep following this street and you should end up at the northern section of Artillery Park.

PARC DE L'ARTILLERIE (ARTILLERY PARK)

The **Parc de l'Artillerie ⑱ (Artillery Park**; www.pc.gc.ca/en/lhn-nhs/qc, fortifications; buildings daily mid-May to early Oct daily 9.30am–5pm; $7.90 marks the northwest corner of Québec's city walls and contains the Officers' Quarters, furnished as it was in 1830, and the

Basilique-Cathédrale Notre-Dame de Québec

massive **Dauphine Redoubt** ⑲, which was completed by the French in 1748. The latter typifies the changes of fortune here: used by the French as the barracks for their garrison, it became the officers' mess under the British and then the residence of the superintendent of the Arsenal. The southern section of the park contains the **Arsenal Foundry** ⑳, completed in 1903, and houses an interpretation centre and a detailed scale model of Québec City.

PORTE ST-JEAN

Just to the south of Artillery Park stands **Porte St-Jean** ㉑ (St. John Gate), a dramatic replica gateway through the city walls in 1939. From here you can stroll back up busy Rue Saint-Jean to get back to the centre, stopping at **Chocolato Vieux-Québec** (https://chocolato.ca) at No. 1015 for a well-earned ice cream, or at celebrated **Chez Boulay** (see ❹) for dinner.

Food and Drink

❶ SMITH CAFÉ (LA MAISON SMITH)
23 rue Notre-Dame; tel: 581-742 6777; https://smithcafe.com; daily 7am–7pm; $
This popular local café mini-chain knocks out decent espressos and lattes from coffee freshly roasted on the Île d'Orléans, as well as hot chocolate, teas and a range of light bites. The outdoor patio is a great spot to take in the scene on Place-Royale.

❷ CHEZ JULES
24 rue Ste-Anne; tel: 418-694 7000; https://chezjules.ca; Mon–Fri 7.30am–10am, 11.30am–1.30pm and 5.30–10pm; Sat–Sun 7.30am–10pm and 5.30–10pm; $$
You're spoiled for choice at this lively French brasserie. The superb menu includes exquisitely prepared items such as sole fillet with rice, a sumptuous croque-madame and duck foie gras. Not a place to skip dessert, particularly the heavenly crème brûlée.

❸ BAGUETTE & CHOCOLAT
36 Côte de la Fabrique; tel: 418-694 7007; www.facebook.com/baguetteetchoco; daily 7.30am–7pm; $
Baguette & Chocolat is a small, modern café serving quality illy coffee and a wonderful selection of pastries, as well as cannoli, excellent crêpes, waffles, sorbets, sandwiches and cookies. They also serve cold beers and vegan alternatives.

❹ CHEZ BOULAY
1110 rue Saint-Jean; tel: 418-380 8166; https://chezboulay.com; Wed–Fri 11.30am–2pm and 5–10pm, Sat–Sun 10am–2pm and 5–10pm; $$$
Lauded restaurant from celebrity chef Jean-Luc Boulay and Arnaud Marchand, specializing in Quebec "boreal" cuisine inspired by the forage-heavy Nordic restaurant movement. Think smoked bison breast, roasted squash and gnocchi in a turnip and nettle pesto with hazelnuts.

ÎLE D'ORLÉANS LOOP

Poised in the middle of the St Lawrence River, and an easy day-trip from Québec City, the wonderfully bucolic Île d'Orléans maintains the flavour of 18th-century French Canada, studded with old stone churches, vineyards, pretty villages, lavender farms, cider mills, jam makers and fromageries.

DISTANCE: 96km

TIME: A full day

START/END: Québec City

POINTS TO NOTE: This tour is designed as a road-trip – cars are easy to rent Québec City. It's recommended in summer; most of the sights on this route close completely or partially from October to May, though the roads themselves are usually open year-round. Always check opening times in advance as seasonal changes can alter the times listed below (as can on-going COVID-19 restrictions). It's best to reserve dinner at Les Ancêtres in advance.

The Île d'Orléans was only joined to the mainland in 1935, when a suspension bridge was constructed from Hwy-440, opposite the Montmorency Falls, connecting it to the west end of the island. Today tourism and agriculture are mainstays: roadside stalls heave under the weight of fresh fruit (especially raspberries and apples), vegetables, jams, dairy products, home-made bread and maple syrup, and the island's restaurants and B&Bs are some of the best in the province.

Encircling the island, Rte-368 – called the Chemin Royal for most of its length – dips and climbs over gentle slopes and terraces past acres of neat farmland and orchards, passing through six villages with their churches evenly spaced around the island's periphery. A counter-clockwise tour of the island is described below.

SAINTE-PÉTRONILLE

Once you've crossed the Pont de l'Île, turn right (west or "ouest") where Rte-368 splits in two and stop at the **Tourist Information Center ❶** on the corner (https://tourisme.iledorleans. com; Jan–Mar, Nov and Dec Mon–Fri 8.30am–4.30pm; Apr and mid-Oct to end Oct Mon–Fri 8.30am–4.30pm, Sat–Sun 11am–3pm; May to mid-June and Sept to mid-Oct Mon–Fri 8.30am–4.30pm, Sat–Sun 9am–5pm; mid-June to Aug daily 8.30am–6pm). From here it's 4km to the island's oldest and most beautifully situated settlement, riverside **Sainte-Pétronille ❷**, characterized

The Montmorency Falls

by the grand white clapboard homes of the merchants who made their fortunes trading farm produce with Québec City. At the heart of the village lie the mouth-watering treats of the **Chocolaterie de l'Ile d'Orleans ❸** (https://chocolaterieorleans.com; see website for seasonal hours), while some of the best views of Québec City and the Montmorency Falls can be had from nearby **Rue Horatio-Walker**, which runs along the riverside promenade. Known unofficially as the "grand seigneur" of Sainte-Pétronille, artist Horatio Walker lived here from 1904 until his death in 1938.

SAINT-LAURENT

From Sainte-Pétronille it's around 12km on the Chemin Royal to the village of **Saint-Laurent**, on the southeastern side of the island. Until the 1950s the south shore was the domain of sailors and navigators, with the village of Saint-Laurent being the island's supplier of *chaloupes*, the long rowing boats that were the islanders' only means of getting to the mainland before the bridge was built.

Today Saint-Laurent is more notable for its art galleries, a couple of tiny roadside chapels (the "**Chapelle de procession**" common on the island, often used here as galleries) and the 1860s **Église de Saint-Laurent** (open daily mid-May to Sept), picturesquely situated right beside the river with a handsome interior created by the architect Charles Baillargé.

La Forge à Pique-Assaut

On the western edge of the village stands **La Forge à Pique-Assaut ❹** (2200 chemin Royale; www.forge-pique-assaut.com/default.htm#; June to mid-Oct daily 9am–5pm; rest of year Mon–Fri 9am–noon and 1.30–5pm; free), a blacksmith's shop with an 18th-century bellows manned by French-born metalworker Guy Bel, a small museum and shop selling forged metal crafts.

Parc Maritime de Saint-Laurent

On the waterfront in the heart of the village lies the **Parc Maritime de Saint-Laurent** (http://parcmaritime.ca; mid-June to mid-Oct daily 10am–5pm; $5), where you can take a guided tour to learn about the island's shipbuilding history and peruse the exhibits in the interpretation centre.

CONFITURERIE TIGIDOU (TIGIDOU JAM FACTORY)

Just under 7km up the road from Saint-Laurent, make a stop at the **Confiturerie Tigidou ❺** (5508 chemin Royal; www.tigidou.ca; see website for seasonal hours), which sells high-quality homemade berry jams throughout the summer (free jam-tasting, or $2 with a scone).

SAINT-JEAN

The prettiest village on the island is **Saint-Jean ❻** (6km northeast of Tigidou). The cemetery of the red-roofed,

Farm summer landscape

18th-century **Eglise de Saint-Jean** contains gravestones of numerous mariners. Grab a coffee and a simple lunch at **La Bolange** (see ❶) near here, which has stellar views of the river.

Manoir Mauvide-Genest

Saint-Jean's museum of antique furniture and domestic objects is housed in the stately **Manoir Mauvide-Genest** (4818 chemin Royal; www.manoir mauvidegenest.com; mid-May to mid-June and mid-Sept to mid-Oct Sat–Sun 11am–5pm; late June to early Sept daily 11am–5pm; $10), a huge mansion built between 1734 and 1752 for ship's surgeon and later "seigneur de l'île d'Orléans" Jean Mauvide. The metre-thick walls withstood the impact from Wolfe's bombardment in 1759 – you can still see dents in the wall.

SAINT-FRANÇOIS

The northermost village of **Saint-François ❽**, 11km northeast of Saint-Jean, is best known for **La Seigneurie ❿** (https://seigneurieiledorleans.com; mid-May to early Oct; $7–20) a fragrant lavender farm and varied gardens that offer guided tours (lavender best in July; tours from $38); and its wooden observation tower (**Tour d'observation St-François ❾**), providing clear views (via 98 steps) of the smaller river islands to the north.

SAINTE-FAMILLE

Beyond Saint-François, the Chemin Royale cuts across the top of the island and loops back towards the southwest. After around 8km you'll hit **Sainte-Famille ❿**, which straggles along the hilltop

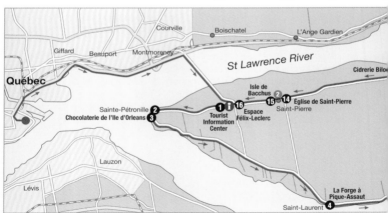

The Île-d'Orléans bridge   *Seigneurie d'Ile-d'Orléans*

ather than the river. Among the French wood and stone buildings here two particularly fine examples are open to the public, the Maison de nos Aïeux and Maison Drouin.

Maison Drouin and Fromages de l'isle d'Orléans

The **Maison Drouin** ⓫ was acquired by the Drouin family in 1872. Today it contains exhibits on the architecture of the island's early houses and is very evocative of colonial Québec. Next door be sure to visit **Les Fromages de l'isle d'Orléans** (www.fromagesdeliledorleans. com; check the website for seasonal hours), where you can see traditional cheese-making and sample artisanal cheeses. Look out for viewpoints of the river along the road here – the Basilique de Sainte-Anne-de-Beaupré (see page

76) should be clearly visible on the far bank of the St Lawrence.

Maison de nos Aïeux

Some 6km further along the road, next to the ornate 18th-century **Église Sainte-Famille**, the 1896 rectory is now the handsome **Maison de nos Aïeux** ⓬ (2485 chemin Royal; www.fondationfran coislamy.com; Mar to late June Sun–Thu 10am–4pm; late June to early Sept daily 10am–5pm; early Sept to mid-Oct daily 10am–4pm; $5).

SAINT-PIERRE

The last village on the loop is also the largest on the island, **Saint-Pierre,** which like Sainte-Famille runs along the hilltops for several kilometres. Around 9km from Maison de nos Aïeux you'll pass **Cidre-**

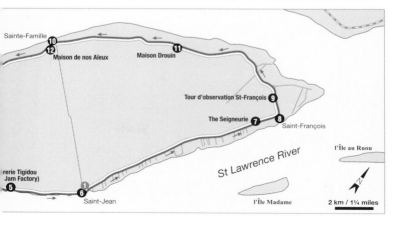

Sainte-Famille par[

rie Bilodeau ⑬ (1868 chemin Royal; https://cidreriebilodeau.com; daily: Mar and Apr 10am–4pm; May–Sept 9am–6pm; Oct–Dec 10am–5pm) a family-run apple orchard and cider mill (which also sells apple butter and sugar pie). Around 4km further on stands the stone **Église de Saint-Pierre** ⑭ (June to early Oct 10am–4pm), the oldest church in rural Québec. Constructed in 1718, it has pews with special hot-brick holders for keeping bottoms warm on seats, while Thomas Baillairgé worked on the interior in the 19th century. A modern church was built next door in 1955. A short drive from here (half a kilometre) is **Isle de Bacchus** ⑮ (1335 chemin Royal; www.isledebacchus.com; Mar and Apr Thu–Sun 11am–5pm, May daily 11am–5pm; June to mid-Oct 10am–6pm), one of several island vineyards that produces an excellent series of ice wines.

Espace Félix-Leclerc

By the time you reach the **Espace Félix-Leclerc** ⑯ (1214 chemin Royal; https://felixleclerc.com; mid-May to early Oct daily 9.30am–5.30pm; $8) near the turning back to the mainland, it's likely to be closed, so if you're a fan of Leclerc make this your first stop after the Tourist Information Center and re-join the tour from here.

Saint-Pierre is celebrated in Québec as the long-time home and final resting place of **Félix Leclerc**, the poet and singer-songwriter who penned *P'tit Bonheur* and the first musician to bring Québécois music international acclaim. The Espace Félix-Leclerc pays homage to Leclerc's life and work, and has several hiking trails and picnic tables. From here it's around 15km to Québec City centre. Alternatively, have dinner on the island at the fabulous **Les Ancêtres** (see ②).

Food and Drink

① LA BOLANGE

4624 chemin Royal, Saint-Jean; tel: 418-829 3162; www.laboulange.ca; Apr and early Oct–Dec Fri–Sat 7.30am–5.30pm; May–late June Thu–Sat 7.30am–5.30pm; late June–Aug Mon–Sat 7.30am–5.30pm; Sept–early Oct Wed–Sat 7.30am–5.30pm; year-round Sun 7.30am–5pm; $
One of the island's best *boulangeries* and justifiably popular, with irresistible bread, pastries and pizzas. Stock up for a picnic or savour the baked goods on the terrace with views of the river.

② LES ANCÊTRES

1101 chemin Royal, Saint-Pierre; tel: 418-828 2718; www.lesancetres.ca; usually open 4–10pm; $$$
Beautiful old farmhouse with open terraces and glass-enclosed dining room offering wonderful views across the St Lawrence. The traditional menu might include goose *rillets* with rutabaga chutney, meatballs and pork hock ragout, and braised Québec lamb shank.

Saint-Siméon surroundings

CÔTE-DE-BEAUPRÉ AND THE CHARLEVOIX

Stretching along the northern bank of the St Lawrence River from Québec City, this route takes in the best of the Côte-de-Beaupré and Charlevoix regions, from Montmorency Falls to the most mesmerizing canyon in eastern Canada.

DISTANCE: 348km
TIME: 3 days
START: Québec City
END: Saint-Siméon (Saguenay Loop)
POINTS TO NOTE: This tour is designed as a road-trip – cars are easy to rent in Québec City. At its southern end the route can be extended with walking tours around Québec City (see page 54) and the Île d'Orléans Loop (see page 68); at its northern terminus, the route links up with the Saguenay Loop (see page 80). Note that although many sights on the route close completely or partially from September to May, the roads themselves are usually open year-round and much of the region comes alive with winter sports and activities at that time. For information on Mont-Sainte-Anne, which isn't included in this tour, see page 102; for accommodation see page 109.

"Oh! What beautiful meadows!" French sailors are supposed to have mur-mured these words whilst admiring the St Lawrence River coast in the 16th century, and today the Côte-de-Beaupré region remains incredibly scenic, stretching from Montmorency Falls to Canyon Sainte-Anne. Also here is the gigantic Basilique de Sainte-Anne-de-Beaupré, which attracts millions of pilgrims annually and is one of the most impressive sites in Québec. There are two roads along the coast: the speedy autoroute Dufferin-Mont-morency (Hwy-440, then Hwy-138) and the slower Avenue Royale (Rte-360), aka the "Route de la Nouvelle-France" (identified with signs illustrating the coat of arms of New France). This tour follows the latter road, which gives a far better introduction to rural life in the province, passing through little villages with ancient farmhouses and churches lining the way. North of Beaupré, the region of Charlevoix, named after the Jesuit historian François Xavier de Charlevoix, comprises gently slop-ing hills, sheer cliffs and vast valleys veined with rivers, brooks and water-falls. It's a landscape that Québec's

Interior of Ste-Anne-de-Beaupre Basilica

better-known artists – Clarence Gagnon, Marc-Aurèle Fortin and Jean-Paul Lemieux – chose for inspiration. Though Charlevoix has been a tourist destination for years, the landscape has been carefully preserved, and quaint villages and historic churches still nestle in an unspoiled countryside.

PARC DE LA CHUTE-MONTMORENCY

Get an early start for the 12km drive from Québec City to **Parc de la Chute-Montmorency ❶** (www.sepaq.com/destinations/parc-chute-montmorency; site open year-round, see website for sea-sonal opening times for facilities; $6.96; parking $3.48 per car; cable car $14.57 return). Here the waters of the Montmorency River cascade 83m down from the Laurentians into the St Lawrence River, making the spectacular Montmorency Falls one and a half times the height of Niagara (though the volume of water is considerably less).

From the main car park a **cable car** runs to the interpretation centre in the **Manoir Montmorency**. The elegant mansion was rebuilt after a fire in 1993 to replicate the 1780 original built by British governor Frederick Haldimand as a country retreat. The interpretation centre chronicles the

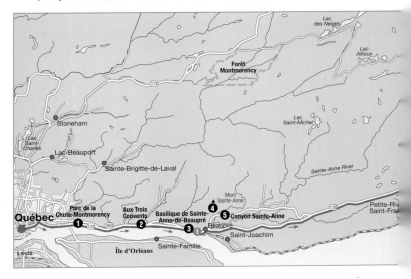

Baie Saint Paul old mill

Basilica of Sainte-Anne-de-Beaupre

history of the site, which includes a period of residence by Queen Victoria's father in the 1790s. From the centre, a cliffside walkway leads to the suspension bridge over the falls and onto the zigzag staircase down the other side, offerings sensational views of the cascade, the St Lawrence River, and l'Île-d'Orléans. Along the way a 300-metre zipline ($28) and via ferrata (from $34) are offered in the summer.

AU TROIS COUVENTS

Aim to leave Montmorency to be in Sainte-Anne-de-Beaupré for lunch and make time for **Aux Trois Couvents ❷**

("the three convents"; 7976 av Royale, Château-Richer; https://aux troiscouvents.org; daily 10am–4pm, closed Jan; $6), which serves as a modest gateway to the Côte-de-Beaupré. Located 15km northeast of Montmorency in the sleepy village of Château-Richer, inside the three-storey building are bilingual exhibits chronicling the history of the Côte-de-Beaupré from the arrival of the first French families in the 1630s. Château-Richer is otherwise known for its fabulous chocolate shop, **Praline & Chocolat** (7874 av Royale; www.pralinechocolat.ca; Mon–Wed 9am–6pm, Thu–Sat 8am–6pm; Sun

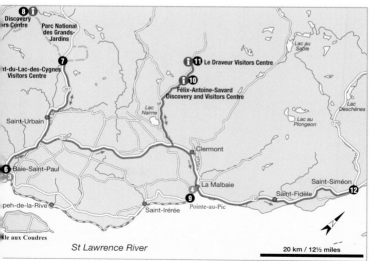

8am–5pm). Continuing north along the Avenue Royale you'll pass the **Atelier Paré** (9269 av Royale; mid-May to mid-Oct daily 9am–5pm; rest of year Wed–Sun 1–4pm; free) just before Sainte-Anne-de-Beaupré, a fascinating workshop and museum of traditional wood carvings.

BASILIQUE DE SAINTE-ANNE-DE-BEAUPRÉ

Some 8km further along Avenue Royale from Au Trois Couvents stands Québec's equivalent of Lourdes – the **Basilique de Sainte-Anne-de-Beaupré** ❸ (https://sanctuairesainte anne.org/en; daily: May–Aug 7am–9.30pm, Sept 8am–5.30pm; Oct–Apr 8.30am–5pm). It dominates the small community of Sainte-Anne-de-Beaupré and the entire area, its twin spires soaring above the St Lawrence shore. The church began in 1658 as a small wooden chapel devoted to St Anne (traditionally the Virgin Mary's mother). The current Romanesque Revival is the fifth church to stand here (consecreated only in 1976), fires and floods having destroyed the first four. The basilica seats 1500, though on St Anne's feast day (July 26) up to 5,000 crowd in. Most of its mesmerizing decoration depicts the miraculous powers of St Anne. Behind the ornate golden statue of St Anne is a chapel said to contain a portion of Anne's forearm, donated by the pope in 1960. Those

who have been cured by her intervention have left a vast collection of crutches and wooden limbs hanging on the basilica's pillars near the entrance.

Be sure to visit the basement **Chapelle de l'Immaculée Conception**, adorned with paintings of the saints, and the small but beautifully decorated **Chapelle du Très-Saint-Sacrement**. Have lunch at the **Microbrasserie Des Beaux Prés** (see ❶), on the main highway not far from the basilica. From here it's short drive up to **Mont-Sainte-Anne** ❹ – if you want to detour here see page 102

CANYON SAINTE-ANNE

From Sainte-Anne-de-Beaupré drive 10km to **Canyon Sainte-Anne** ❺ (http://canyonsa.qc.ca; mid-May to late June and early Sept to mid-Oct daily 9am–5pm; late June to early Sept daily 9am–6pm; $14.50) an especially grand waterfall – here the Saint Anne River has carved a gorge where the water tumbles 74m, flanked by a chasm fringed with woodlands and short nature trails. A bridge crosses just before the precipice, giving views down the canyon, while in front of the falls a suspension bridge allows for splendid and terrifying views.

Project Vertical (https://proje vertical.com) leads a variety of adrenaline-fuelled activities in the canyon including a thrilling 60m zip-line over

Suspension Bridge over the Canyon Sainte-Anne

the gorge and a challenging via ferrata climb, also open in the winter. When you're done, continue 54km northeast on Rte-138 to **Baie St Paul** ❻, where there's plenty of accommodation. Family-friendly **Joe Smoked Meat** (see ❷), is a solid option for dinner, while **Le Saint-Pub** (2 rue Racine; www.saint-pub.com) is a convivial spot for a drink or two.

DAY 2: BAIE-SAINT-PAUL

Spend the morning of day two exploring picture-perfect **Baie St Paul**, one of the earliest settlements in Charlevoix and long-time gathering place for Québec's landscape painters. Dominated by the twin spires of the **Église de Baie-Saint-Paul** (the fifth church to stand here, inaugurated in 1964), winding streets radiate out from the Rivière Gouffré, flanked by houses that are more than 200 years old.

From beside the church, the main road **Rue St-Jean-Baptiste** slips through the commercial heart of the town edged by numerous quaint cottages characteristic of Québec's earliest houses, with curving roofs and wide verandas, many converted into commercial galleries.

The gallery in the aging **Maison de René-Richard** (58 Rue St-Jean-Baptiste, entrance on Rue Clarence Gagnon; daily 11am–6pm; free) offers an insight into the works of René Richard, an associate of the Group of Seven.

The 1852 house has been left exactly the same since Richard died in 1982.

Musée d'art contemporain de Baie-Saint-Paul

For an overview of the works of art produced in Charlevoix, visit the plush **Musée d'art contemporain de Baie-Saint-Paul** (23 rue Ambroise-Fafard;

Mont-Sainte-Anne

Just up the highway from Sainte-Anne-de-Beaupré is the town of Beaupré, which provides access to Mont-Sainte-Anne (https://mont-sainte-anne.com). Centred on a single peak, it's easily navigable yet still provides a remarkably varied high-density trail system. The resort's greatest strength is its wealth of intermediate-level runs that make up almost half the ski zone. The ski resort is also an off-season destination; in summer you can explore the extensive cross-country mountain-bike trails; bikes can be rented at the base area. Hikers wanting to enjoy the remarkable views over the St Lawrence River can take the gondola up the mountain. Yet one of the best hiking trails leaves out of the car park at the base area – head down the hill and over the bridge along the main road – to the Chutes Jean-Larouse, a 20-minute walk. The trail leads to a series of dramatic waterfalls, though the stairway alongside it is just as dizzyingly impressive.

Le Manoir Richelieu

www.macbsp.com; late June to early Sept daily 10am–5pm; early Sept to late June Tue–Sun 11am–5pm; $10), which has an international reputation for the excellence of its temporary exhibitions of Québécois and international paintings, sculpture and photography in particular.

Walk around the corner for lunch and coffee at **Café Charlevoix** (see ❸).

PARC NATIONAL DES GRANDS-JARDINS

Spend the afternoon in beautiful **Parc national des Grands-Jardins** (www.sepaq.com/pq/grj; Mont-du-Lac visitor centre hours vary but generally daily: June–Aug 8.30am–8pm; Sept, Oct and Mar–May 9am–4pm; Nov–Feb 9am–4pm Sat–Sun only; $8.90), 32km inland from Baie-Saint-Paul via Rte-381. Start at the **Mont-du-Lac-des-Cygnes Visitors Centre** ❼ on Rte-381 (km 21), where there's information on trails, ranging from the intermediate 4.8km **La Chouenne Trail** (2hr) to a series of easy woodland paths starting at the **Arthabaska Discovery and Visitors Centre** ❽ (open late May to mid-Oct only, daily 9am–8pm), some 19km further into the park. From Mont-du-Lac drive 64km (via routes 381 and 138) to your overnight stop at **Pointe-au-Pic** ❾ (allow one hour), in La Malbaie. Aim to have dinner at **Restaurant L'Orchidée** (see ❹).

DAY 3: POINTE-AU-PIC

The ritzy resort area **Pointe-au-Pic** back on the St Lawrence shore forms part of **La Malbaie**, an amalgamation of five riverside villages that has been a popular summer retreat since the 19th century. Take a look at the grand **Le Manoir Richelieu** (see page 109) originally built in 1899 then reconstructed in French château-style in 1929 after a fire. History buffs might also want to have a peek inside the **Musée de Charlevoix** (10 chemin du Havre; www.museedecharlevoix.qc.ca June to mid-Oct daily 9am–5pm; mid-Oct to May Tue–Fri 10am–5pm, Fri–Sat 10am–4pm; $8), which provides a small overview of the region. Buy food for a picnic at Provigo (25 blvd Kane daily 8am–9pm) and aim to spend the rest of the day in the **Parc national des Hautes-Gorges-de-la-Rivière-Malbaie**, 40km inland up the Malbaie River valley.

PARC NATIONAL DES HAUTES-GORGES-DE-LA-RIVIÈRE-MALBAIE

The **Parc national des Hautes-Gorges-de-la-Rivière-Malbaie** (www.sepaq.com/pq/hgo/index.dot?language_id=1; $8.60) is a network of valleys slicing through a maze of lofty peaks. As you enter the park, cliff faces on all sides rise up to more than 700m, making it Canada's deepest

Hautes-Gorges-de-la-Rivière-Malbaie

canyon east of the Rockies. Its unique-ness lies not just in this astounding geology but also in the fact that all of Québec's forest species grow in this one comparatively small area. The **Félix-Antoine-Savard Discovery and Visitors Centre** ⑩ (late May to Nov), is located beside the river, just off the main road into the park.

Rent a bike into the park as far as the **Le Draveur Visitors Centre** ⑪

(open Dec to mid-Oct; Sat–Sun only Dec–Apr).

The best way to take the park's nat-ural bounty is by hiking; short and easy trails fan out from Le Draveur, and you can also take boat tours and go kay-aking. From the Félix-Antoine-Savard centre it's 73km to **Saint-Siméon** ⑫ (takes around 1hr 15min), or 150km back to Québec City (takes at least two hours).

Food and Drink

① MICROBRASSERIE DES BEAUX PRÉS

9430 blvd Ste-Anne (Rte-138), Sainte-Anne-de-Beaupré; tel: 418-702 1128; https://mdbp.ca; Tue 3–10pm, Wed noon–11pm, Thu and Sat noon–midnight, Fri noon–1am, Sun noon–10pm; $$

By far the most enticing option in Saint-Anne itself, this brewpub lies just under 2km from the basilica (20min walk). Try the beef chilli or smoked meat panini, washed down with "Bonne Sainte-Anne" blonde ale or "Route 138" double IPA.

② JOE SMOKED MEAT

54 rue St-Jean-Baptiste, Baie-Saint-Paul; tel: 418-240 4949; https://joesmokedmeat. com; daily 11am–9pm; $$

A menu stocked with hearty dishes at this lively chain restaurant. The signature sandwich, a sub ("sous-marins") stuffed

with smoked meat, steak slices, cheese and peppers is a veritable gut buster.

③ CAFÉ CHARLEVOIX

20 rue Sainte Anne, Baie-Saint-Paul; tel: 418-760 8872; www.cafecharlevoix.ca; daily 8am–3pm; $

Cozy artisanal coffee roasters (all the beans are roasted in Baie-Saint-Paul), with fabulous espressos and cappuccinos, as well as scones, croissants, *viennoiseries*, and bagels.

④ RESTAURANT L'ORCHIDÉE

439 rue Saint Étienne, La Malbaie; tel: 418-665 1070; www.restaulorchidee.com; daily 5.30–9pm (closed Mon and Tue Nov–Apr); $$$

Elegant and romantic restaurant serving refined French and Québécois cuisine, especially known for its chowder, seafood pasta, salmon and beef dishes, especially the *boeuf au jus;* also offers gluten-free options.

Ferry passing across Saguenay river

SAGUENAY LOOP

This route loops the majestic Fjord du Saguenay, which cuts deep into the Québec interior from the St Lawrence River, rimmed by a stupendous expanse of rocky outcrops, sheer cliffs and dense forests – it also takes in placid Lac Saint-Jean, the source of Saguenay.

DISTANCE: 600km

TIME: 3 Days

START: Saint-Siméon

END: Tadoussac

POINTS TO NOTE: This tour is a road-trip, making a long loop around the Fjord du Saguenay from its southern to northern banks; it's designed to connect with the Côte-de-Beaupré and Charlevoix tour at Saint-Siméon (see page 73), and with the Côte-Nord route at Tadoussac (see page 86). It's also possible to complete the tour from Québec City – Saint-Siméon is just over two hours drive from the provincial capital. Note that although many sights on the route close completely or partially from September to May, the roads themselves are usually open year-round and much of the region comes alive with winter sports and activities at that time. Try to reserve all activities and boat rides in the Parc National du Fjord-du-Saguenay in advance. For accommodation options on the route see page 110.

The Fjord du Saguenay is one of the longest fjords in the world, cutting through the Canadian Shield before merging with the St Lawrence River. It's incredibly scenic, the fjord's banks and forests protected by the Parc national du Fjord-du-Saguenay, and the water itself forms part of the Parc marin du Saguenay–Saint-Laurent (https://parcmarin.qc.ca). The marine park contains six different ecosystems and supports hundreds of marine species, including whales. The white St Lawrence River beluga lives in the area year-round, and from May to October it is joined by six species of migratory whale, including the minke, finback and blue. This route makes a loop around the whole fjord, as well as Lac Saint-Jean at the western end and Tadoussac at the mouth of the fjord, the latter best known as a whale-watching hub.

L'ANSE-SAINT-JEAN

Coming from Charlevoix, Rte-170 branches off coastal Rte-138 at **Saint Siméon** ❶, wriggling its way north through the heavily forested interior

Faubourg Bridge 　　　　　　　*View on the Anse–Saint-Jean village*

towards the Fjord du Saguenay. To get your first taste of the **Parc national du Fjord-du-Saguenay**, take the turning after around 68km to **L'Anse-Saint-Jean** ❷, another 6km down the Saint-Jean River valley. The village is famous for its **Pont du Faubourg**, a covered bridge. L'Anse-Saint-Jean also has a terrific view of the fjord and surrounding hills from the marina. Grab a coffee or a snack here at the ideally sited **Café du Quai** (see ❶).

L'Anse-de-Tabatière

Take in the stupendous view of the Saguenay from the **L'Anse-de-Tabatière lookout** ❸, 5.5km further along the coastal road. It's the most beautiful area in the national park accessible by car. Note that you'll have to pay the Parc national du Fjord-du-Saguenay entry fee ($8.90) online and in advance.

PARC NATIONAL DU FJORD-DU-SAGUENAY: BAIE-ÉTERNITÉ

From L'Anse-de-Tabatière continue 28km to the central **Baie-Éternité sector** of the **Parc national du Fjord-du-Saguenay**; the entrance is clearly signposted off Rte-170 in the village of Rivière-Éternité. There's the small **Baie-Éternité Information Kiosk** ❹ (late May to mid-Oct 8am–4pm) here, but the primary **Le Fjord du Saguenay Discovery and Visitors Centre** ❺ (late May to mid-Oct 8am–4pm) is 7.5km further along the road on the fjord itself. Aim to spend the rest of the day here: you can buy snacks

and drinks at the Visitors Centre, but you could also stock up with picnic supplies at one of the grocery stores back in Rivière-Éternité on Rte-170. Accommodation managed by the park runs from basic campsites to more comfortable "ready-to-camp tents" and comparatively luxurious "Écho cabins", but there is also the decent Auberge du Presbytère back in Rivière-Éternité.

Hiking Trails

From the Discovery and Visitors Centre, a couple of short hikes and a long one branch out through this sector of the park. The easiest is the 1.6km round-trip **Sentier des Méandres-à-Falaises**, but the best trail is the **Sentier de la Statue**, a fairly easy 4hr (7.6km) round-trip up the massive bluff of **Cap Trinité**, which flanks the deep-blue water of the Baie-Éternité. The summit is topped by a huge statue known as **Our Lady of the Saguenay** ❻.

Boat Trips

Try to spend at least some time on the fjord itself – always check times in advance and book ahead if possible. Most boats and activities originate at the Discovery and Visitors Centre. The best overall scenic cruises take place in the **Le Fjord Saguenay II** (www.navettes dufjord.com; from $60), known as the "*bateau-mouche*" thanks to its retractable roof that provides panoramic views. You can also take more exhilarating zodiac rides and kayaking tours (each from $58).

DAY 2: LA BAIE

Get an early start today to once more head west on Rte-170 – from Riv-ière-Eternité it's around 120km (at least 1hr 30min) to vast Lac Saint-Jean, the source of the Fjord du Saguenay. After around 40km, on the edge of **La Baie** ❽, look out for the bizarre sight of a pyramid plated with red and white "Yield" signs. The **Pyramide des Ha! Ha!** ❼ (named after the nearby river) commemorates the tragic Saguenay flood of 1996, in which 10 people lost their lives. The best place for breakfast is **Stop Café** (see ❷), a little further along Rte-170 on the other side of La Baie. Between here and the lake there's not much to see – take Autoroute 70 to bypass most of the industrial sights.

LAC SAINT-JEAN

The huge, glacial **Lac Saint-Jean** ❾ is fed by most of the rivers of northeast-ern Québec and is bordered by sandy beaches and a lush, green terrain that has been farmed for over a century. Many come as well for the local cuisine, especially the delicious coarse meat pie called a *tourtière* and the thick local blueberry pie. It's a relatively untouched area with tranquil lakeshore villages linked by Rte-169, which makes a loop around the whole lake – drive Rte-170 to its western terminus and take Rte-169 clockwise (west) towards Val-Jal-bert. Around 17km beyond the junction of Rte-170 and Rte-169, enjoy the pan-oramic view of the lake at the **Halte Routière de Chambord** ❿.

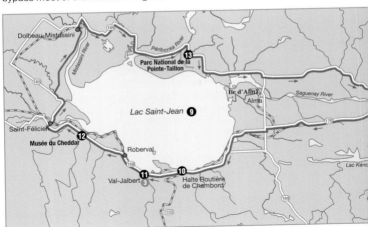

L'Anse-Saint-Jean

Val-Jalbert

The historical village or "ghost-town" of **Val-Jalbert** (www.valjalbert.com/en; daily: late May to mid-June and late Aug to mid-Oct 10am–5pm; mid-June to late Aug 9am–6pm; $36) lies 10km beyond Halte Routière de Chambord. The 72m-high **Ouiatchouan Falls**, south of the town, led to the establishment of a pulp mill here more than a century ago. In 1927 the introduction of chemical-based pulping made the mill redundant, and the village was closed down; in 1985 it was renovated as a tourist attraction. From the site entrance a bus (with on-board French commentary) runs around the main sights of the village. Afterwards, you can wander around the abandoned wooden houses, a former convent (now a museum) or the general store (now a souvenir shop). From the mill (now an excellent crafts market and cafeteria) a pathway with viewpoints leads to the top of the falls, from where there are stunning views of the village and Lac Saint-Jean beyond. Have lunch in the mill at the **Restaurant du Moulin** (see ❸).

Musée du Cheddar

Some 22km on from Val-Jalbert, Saint-Prime village has a surprising little museum, the **Musée du Cheddar** (148 av Albert-Perron; www.museecheddar.org; daily: early to late June and late Aug to late Sept 10am–5pm; late June to late Aug 9.30am–6pm; $16), where four generations of cheese-makers have worked since 1895. The one-hour guided tour covers the whole process of cheddar production (some of which is

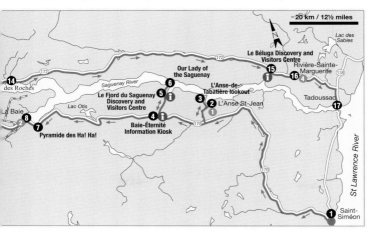

still exported to England). The tour also includes the Perron family residence as it would have appeared in 1922, and samples of the cheese produced by the modern factory.

Parc National de la Pointe-Taillon

From Saint-Prime Rte-169 winds its way inland as it loops around the western end of the lake, a pleasant drive that after around 100km runs back to the water at **Parc National de la Pointe-Taillon** (www.sepaq.com/pq/pta; late May to mid-Oct; $8.90). Stop here to view the lake again and the long and sandy beach behind the Discovery and Visitor Centre – it's a beautiful spot to relax and enjoy the view if the weather's good.

DAY 3: FJORD-DU-SAGUENAY: NORTHERN SHORE

Get another early start for a long drive along the northern side of the Fjord du Saguenay – Rte-172 is a dramatic route along the less-frequented northern shore that gives occasional panoramas over the water and provides access to a couple of pretty towns en route, where cruises are available or kayaks can be rented. Drive around 150km (2hr) to the Baie-Sainte-Marguerite sector of the **Parc national du Fjord-du-Saguenay**. If you want to stretch your legs, stop at the village of **Saint-Fulgence** and follow the well-marked trail to the **Cap des Roches** viewpoint across the fjord. The village also contains the excellent **Microbras-**

serie **Le Saint-Fût** (www.facebook.com lesaintfut) where you can stock up o craft beers.

Baie-Sainte-Marguerite

Re-enter the Parc national du Fjord-d Saguenay Park at the Baie-Sainte-Ma guerite sector, where **Le Bélug Discovery and Visitors Centre** (lat May to early Oct 8am–6pm; $8.90) lie 3km down a side road off Rte-172. Th main draw here the distinctively whit beluga whale; ask at the visitor cen tre desk for an English-language guide book. An easy 3km walk through th woods along the long-distance Sentie le Fjord leads to an observation platform from where the belugas can frequent be spotted; the bay is regularly visite by schools of female whales with the young in July and August.

Rivière-Sainte-Marguerite

As you re-join Rte-172 and head eas you'll drive into the village of **Rivièr Sainte-Marguerite** , worth a quic stop for its covered bridge, **Pont Lou is-Gravel**, and its celebrated lunc shack, **Halte Gourmande "La Friterie** (see).

TADOUSSAC

End the loop at **Tadoussac** (20k from Rivière-Sainte-Marguerite), on of Canada's oldest villages and beaut fully situated at the neck of the Fjord d Saguenay and its confluence with th

Hiking in National Park Fjord Saguenay

st Lawrence River. The waterfront Rue u Bord-de-l'Eau is dominated by the ed roof and green lawns of the **Hôtel adoussac**, a landmark since 1864 and he focus of the historic quarter.

Across the road is the oldest wooden hurch in Canada, the tiny **Chapelle de adoussac**, built in 1747 and now con-aining a multimedia exhibit on the lives f New France missionaries. Other high-ights here include the **Centre d'Inter-** **prétation des Mammifères Marins**, highly recommended if you intend to go **whale-watching**, and the **Tadoussac dunes** sector of the Parc national du Fjord-du-Saguenay (known locally as "le desert"). For accommodation in Tadous-sac see page 110.

From here traffic crosses the neck of the fjord by a free car ferry to Baie-Sainte-Catherine, 210km from Québec City.

Food and Drink

❶ CAFÉ DU QUAI

358 rue Saint-Jean-Baptiste, L'Anse-Saint-Jean; tel: 418-608 8425; www.cafeduquai.ca; Mon–Thu 11am–4pm, Fri–Sat 11am–9pm, Sun 9am–4pm; $

Overlooking the fjord, this pleasant café is great stop for coffee and especially authentic Breton-style *crêpes*, savoury and sweet. It also does excellent smoked-salmon baguette sandwiches, soups, vegetarian lasagne, cakes and salads.

❷ STOP CAFÉ

2100 rue Bagot, La Baie (inside Les Galeries de la Baie mall); tel: 418-544 8050; Mon–Wed 7am–5.30pm, Thu–Fri 7am–9pm, Sat 8am–5pm, Sun 9am–4pm; $

Old-school diner with a long counter with stools and a handful of tables, in a strip mall just off Rte-170. Great breakfasts: think eggs, toast, bacon, home fries and bottomless coffee. Also do burgers and a variety of desserts.

❸ RESTAURANT DU MOULIN

95 rue Saint-George, Val-Jalbert Historical Village (in the Mill); tel: 418-608 8425; www.cafeduquai.ca; Mon–Thu 11am–4pm, Fri–Sat 11am–9pm, Sun 9am–4pm; $$

Meals in the old mill at Val-Jalbert highlight regional cuisine from Saguenay-Lac-Saint-Jean (incorporating local Perron cheddar cheese, vegetables from the garden chez Lévesque and Boréal Saint-Prime pork). Try the famous *tourtière* meat pie here (they also do burgers and pasta).

❹ HALTE GOURMANDE "LA FRITERIE"

448 Rte-172, Rivière-Sainte-Marguerite; tel: 418-236 9473; http://halte-friterie.edan.io; daily 11am–7pm; $

No-frills outdoor food shacks locally celebrated for its tasty homemade poutine and burgers, plus freshly made lemonade, hot dogs, sandwiches and fries. Eat at the outdoor seating or take-away. Free wi-fi on-site.

THE CÔTE-NORD

Traverse the remote northern St Lawrence coastline on this three-day road-trip, taking in the whale-rich waters of the Haute-Côte-Nord, multimedia Jardin des Glaciers, Innu culture, wild bays, dense boreal forests and pretty fishing villages like Godbout.

DISTANCE: 845km
TIME: 3 days
START: Tadoussac
END: Kegashka
POINTS TO NOTE: This tour is a road-trip, running along the northern bank of the St Lawrence from Tadoussac on Rte-138 – it is designed to link up with the Saguenay Loop (see page 80). Note that most sights on the route close completely from September to May. If you plan to visit the Mingan Archipelago it's crucial to book ferries and accommodation in advance. The information centre for the Côte-Nord is in a red-brick manor at 197 rue des Pionniers in Tadoussac (https://tourismecote-nord.com; daily: late June to early Sept 8am–9pm; early Sept to late June 9am–noon and 1–5pm). For accommodation options on the route see page 86.

The St Lawrence River was the life-line of the wilderness beyond Tadoussac until the 1960s, when Route 138

was constructed along the Côte-Nor to Havre-Saint-Pierre, 625km away and later Kegashka, another 202kr distant. The road sweeps from hig vistas down to the rugged shore line through the vast regions of Mar icouagan and Duplessis. Traditiona sightseeing diversions are thin on th ground in the villages and towns e route, but there is plenty to reward journey to this remote region, not leas the strong Innu and Mi'kmaq herit age and the panorama of spruce-cov ered mountains, the vast sky and th mighty St Lawrence. It is the river tha holds much of what is most alluring i the Côte-Nord, from the striking beaut of the Mingan Archipelago to gazing a the Northern Lights.

LA HAUTE-CÔTE-NORD

North of **Tadoussac ❶**, Rte-138 cut into the **Haute-Côte-Nord** region, wit your first chance to view the immens size of the St Lawrence here at th **Cap de Bon-Désir Interpretation an Observation Centre ❷** ($7.90; mic

Perroquets Island, Mingan Archipelago

June to mid-Oct daily 9am–6pm), 30km along the road. There's a small lighthouse on the cape, and whales can often be seen offshore. Another 8.5km north stands the **Marine Environment Discovery Centre ❸** (mid-June to early Sept daily 9am–6pm; early Sept to early Oct Fri–Sun 9am–5pm; $7.90 – ticket from Cap de Bon-Désir valid here), which highlights the fauna and flora of the Parc Marin du Saguenay–Saint-Laurent. Stop at **Poissonnerie Escoumins** (see ❶), for lunch, a little further on in the village of **Les Escoumins ❹** itself.

BAIE-COMEAU

From Les Escoumins proceed 160km (allow two hours) to the humdrum city of **Baie-Comeau ❺**, worth a visit for **Le Jardin des Glaciers** (3 av Denonville; https://lejardindesglaciers.com; check website for hours; $28). This multimedia show explores glaciers of the last ice age, climate change and the migration of the first humans to reach North America through 3D projections, virtual elevators and sound effects. Check out also out the **Église Sainte-Amélie** (36 av Marquette; daily: late June to early Sept 9am–6pm; free; 15min audio tour $5), for its stunning frescoes and stained-glass windows, designed by the Italian artist Guido Nincheri. Not far from here is **Microbrasserie St-Pancrace–Le Pub** (see ❷), a great place for dinner, and the

Hôtel Le Manoir (see page 110), the best place to stay.

DAY 2: GODBOUT

Get an early start to drive the 57km east on Rte-138 to the attractive village of **Godbout ❻**, situated on a crescent-shaped bay, and the excellent **Musée Amérindien et Inuit** (134 chemin Pascal-Comeau; late June to Sept daily 9am–5pm; by donation). The museum was founded by Claude Grenier, who spent 10 years in the north in the 1970s on a government scheme to boost the Inuit economy by promoting Indigenous culture. Consequent commercialism has diluted the output since then, but the private collection of Grenier features nothing but genuine pieces.

PORT-CARTIER

From here continue around 120km further on Rte-138 to **Port-Cartier ❼**, a mining town and port known for the Aux-Rochers River falls in the centre of town and the adjacent **Pavillon d'interprétation du Saumon** (24 rue Luc-Mayrand; June to mid-Aug daily 10am–7pm; $3), with exhibits on the salmon ladder here. On the west bank of the river lies the **Centre d'interprétation de l'histoire de Port-Cartier** (45 blvd du Portage-des-Mousses; June–Sept daily 9am–6pm; free), which chronicles the complex history of the town. Grab lunch back on Rte-138 at **Restaurant Des Chutes** (see ❸).

Natashquan's fisherman cabin

SEPT-ÎLES

From Port-Cartier continue on Rte-138 for 60km to **Sept-Îles** ❽, named after the seven-island archipelago just off-shore in the Gulf of St Lawrence. The city is now the largest ore-exporting port in eastern Canada, a major alumini-um-processing centre and, in recent years, an unlikely cruise ship desti-nation. The town itself isn't especially attractive, but you can easily spend the afternoon here to visit its muse-ums and historic sites that explore Innu and early fur trading culture. The absorbing **Musée Shaputuan** (290 blvd des Montagnais; late June to early Sept Mon–Fri 8am–4.30pm, Sat–Sun 1–4pm; early Sept to late June Mon–Fri 8am–4.30pm; $5.50) presents the traditional life of the Innu people as

it is shaped by the seasons, while the history of the region is chronicled at the **Musée Régional de la Côte-Nord** (500 blvd Laure; http://museeregional cotenord.ca; late June to early Sept daily 9am–5pm; early Sept to late June Tue–Fri 10am–noon and 1–5pm, Sat–Sun 1–5pm; $7). In the summer **Le Vieux-Poste** (rue Shimun, at the western end of Boulevard des Mon tagnais; http://vieuxposte.com; late June to Aug Mon 10am–5pm, Tue–Sun 10am–6pm; $12) comes alive as a recreation of a fur trading post in the 19th century, with costumed interpret ers, timber trading desk, an interactive exhibition explaining the history of the site and an Innu encampment. For din ner, head to **Casse-Croûte du Pêcheur** (see ❹), then walk along the riverfront promenade (Parc du Vieux-Quai), where

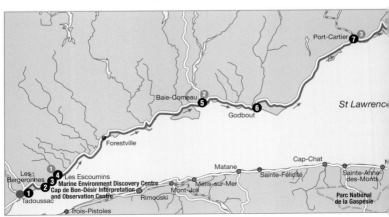

American Dunlin

Hotel le Manoir

evening concerts of Québécois music are held (late June to late Aug; free). For accommodation see page 110.

DAY 3: THE MINGAN COAST

There is little of specific interest along the stretch of shore east of Sept-Îles, known as the Mingan coast until you reach **Havre-Saint-Pierre**, but the scenery changes dramatically with sand dunes followed by granite outcroppings of the Canadian Shield, then eerie landscapes of rounded grey boulders surrounded by scrubby vegetation. Most visitors make the journey for the stunning islands of the **Mingan Archipelago** ⑩, a unique environment of sculptured rock formations and profuse wildlife lying off the coast – this route doesn't take in the archipelago, but it's worth carving out a

few days for the islands if you can (see www.pc.gc.ca/en/pn-np/qc/mingan).

Havre-Saint-Pierre

From Sept-Îles continue 220km due east along Rte-138 to the community of **Havre-Saint-Pierre** ⑨, overlooking the densely wooded islands of the **Réserve de parc national de l'Archipel-de-Mingan**. Founded in 1857 by fleeing Acadians, Saint-Pierre would have remained a tiny fishing village but for the discovery in the 1940s of a huge deposit of ilmenite, the chief source of titanium. The quarries are 45km north of town, where fishing and tourism provide employment for the non-miners, the latter industry having received a major boost when the 40 Mingan islands were made into a national park in 1983. Check out the national

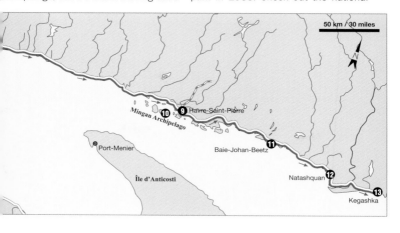

Monoliths from the Archipelago of Minga

park **Reception and Interpretation Center** (mid-June to early Sept daily

Basse Côte-Nord trip

From **Kegashka**, access further up the Basse Côte-Nord is by snowmobile (in winter), floatplane or boat. The *M/V Bella Desgagnés* (mid-Apr to mid-Jan; http://relaisnordik.com) makes a weekly journey here on a trip that affords stunning views of a rocky, subarctic landscape so cold that icebergs occasionally float past the ship even in the height of summer. The boat is evenly split between its role as a freighter and passenger ship; the majority of its passengers are locals skipping between settlements or heading for a longer jaunt to Québec's bigger towns. Its voyage begins in **Rimouski** on Monday nights, stopping in **Sept-Îles** and **Port-Menier** on Île d'Anticosti on Tuesdays and **Havre-Saint-Pierre** and **Natashquan** on Wednesdays before calling in at the roadless communities along the Basse Côte-Nord, reaching **Blanc-Sablon**, Québec's most easterly village on the Labrador border, on Fridays. The same route is then followed in reverse to arrive back in Rimouski on Monday morning.

The journey up this stretch of the St Lawrence is far more impressive than the destinations. During the day, whales, dolphins, seals and a wealth of sea birds are a common sight; at night the **Northern Lights** often present an unforgettable display.

8am–7.30pm), which shares a building with the tourist office on the wharf at 1010 promenade des Anciens. The centre has displays and information on the flora, fauna and geology of the islands.

BASSE CÔTE-NORD

Rte-138 used to end at Havre-Saint Pierre, leaving the dozen or so villages along the rugged **Basse Côte-Nord** (Lower North Shore) cut off from the rest of Québec, as they had been for centuries. Since 2013 Rte-138 has linked Havre-Saint-Pierre with Kegashka, with the rest of the coast accessible by boat. If you make the last leg of this lonely journey you will receive a welcome unique to a people not long connected by road to the rest of Canada.

Baie-Johan-Beetz

Some 67km east of Havre-Saint-Pierre the village of **Baie-Johan-Beetz** ❶ was named after the painter and sculptor whose extraordinary and enormous house built in 1897, **La Pourvoirie Baie Johan-Beetz** (www.pourvoiries.com), is open to the public as hotel and restaurant – aim to have lunch here if you can.

Natashquan

A further 83km from Baie-Johan-Beetz, a small church, wooden houses and the old weather-worn huts of cod fishermen ("**Les Galets**") are about all there is to **Natashquan** ❷, one-time home of revered Québécois poet **Gilles Vig**

Old lighthouse in Longue-Pointe-de-Mingan

neault. **La Vieille École** (24 chemin d'en Haut; late June to early Sept daily 10.30am–noon and 1.30–4.30pm; $5). A schoolhouse built in the early 20th century (and which Vigneault attended) proudly displays memorabilia from his life's works.

Kegashka

Drive the final 48km of Rte-138 to the small fishing village of **Kegashka** ⑬, and you've really reached the end of the road. Located between two tranquil bays and on an island, connected by bridge to the mainland, the village is best known for its white sand beaches and hiking trails covered with crushed shells. Most of the villagers make a living from crab, lobster and scallop fishing. It's an incredibly atmospheric place to end your journey, though it is possible to continue by boat (see page 90), and the road is likely to be extended in the coming years – watch this space.

Food and Drink

① POISSONNERIE ESCOUMINS

152 rue Marcellin Est, Les Escoumins; tel: 418-233 3122; www.fruitsdemeretpoissons. com; Mon–Thu and Sun 8am–8pm, Fri 11am–9pm, Sat 8am–9pm; $$
An essential stop for fish and seafood lovers, this cavernous cafeteria-style restaurant prepares dishes that couldn't be fresher; the tasty clam chowder and seafood pie are easily worth a stop alone. The prices are very reasonable, and there's terrace seating and free wi-fi, too.

② MICROBRASSERIE ST-PANCRACE– LE PUB

55 place la Salle, Baie-Comeau; tel: 418-296 0099; https://microbrasserie.stpancrace. com; Mon–Thu 3–9pm, Fri–Sun 1–11pm; $$
This local craft brewery and pub comes as a pleasant surprise in sleepy Baie-Comeau, with dishes such as Angus burgers, salmon pizza, and smoked meat poutine accompanied by excellent beers, wine, whisky and cocktails.

③ RESTAURANT DES CHUTES

24 rue des Chutes, Port-Cartier; tel: 418-766 2787; Mon–Fri 11am–9pm, Sat–Sun 8am–9pm; $
No frills roadside diner offering typical comfort food, from pizza and burgers to smoked ham sandwiches, delicious poutines and chicken and chips.

④ CASSE-CROÛTE DU PÊCHEUR

4 rue Maltais, Sept-Îles; tel: 418-968 6411; June to early Sept daily 11am–8pm; $$
Fabulous seafood restaurant right on the marina (with its own mini-lighthouse/gift shop), with piles of fresh crab, lobster and an incredible "poutine de la mer" (fries smothered in a creamy seafood sauce crammed with shrimp).

BAS-SAINT-LAURENT (ROUTE DES NAVIGATEURS)

This route covers the southern banks of the mighty St Lawrence north of Québec City, taking in local woodcarvers, grand historic estates and riverine national parks rich in wildlife, as well as the chance to go whale-watching in the summer.

DISTANCE: 320km
TIME: 3 Days
START: Québec City
END: Rimouski (Pointe-au-Père)
POINTS TO NOTE: This tour is a road-trip, running along the southern bank of the St Lawrence from Québec City – it is designed to link up with the Gaspé Peninsula Loop (see page 97) at Rimouski, and can also been combined with other routes originating in Québec City. Note that most sights on the route close completely or partially from September to June. The main information centre for the Bas-Saint-Laurent region is in Rivière-du-Loup at 189 blvd l'Hôtel-de-Ville (www.bassaintlaurent.ca; late June to early Sept Mon–Fri 9am–5pm, Sat 10am–4pm; rest of year Mon–Fri 8.30am–4.30pm, closed for lunch). Reserve all boat trips at Rivière-du-Loup and Kamouraska in advance. For accommodation, see page 111.

East from Québec City, the southern shore of the St Lawrence is known as the Bas-Saint-Laurent (Lower St Lawrence), a region of fertile lands with farming and forestry covering gently rolling hills. The landscape is agricultural and dominated by long, narrow fields that are remnants of the old seigneurial system. The fast Autoroute-20 zips you out of Metro Québec City, but thereafter the most scenic route is Rte 132, which sticks close to the shoreline, aka **Route des Navigateurs**. It takes in the woodcarving centre of Saint-Jean-Port-Joli, the seigneurial Saint-Roch-des-Aulnaies, the architecturally quaint Kamouraska, the regional centre of Rivière-Du-Loup and the stunning coastal landscapes of Parc national du Bic.

L'ISLET

Some 105km northeast from Québec City (take exit 400 from Autoroute 20), stop at the beautiful community of **L'Islet** to visit the impressive **Musée Maritime du Québec ❶** (55 chemin des Pionniers Est; www.mmq.qc.ca; Mar–May Wed–Sun 10am–4pm, June daily

Parc national du Bic

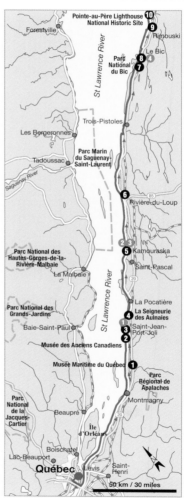

10am–5pm, July to Labour Day daily 10am–6pm, Labour Day to Thanksgiving Tue–Sun 10am–4pm; $14). The museum chronicles Québec's long relationship with the sea, with a boathouse containing historic ships, 200 scale models of watercraft and a variety of exhibits exploring the lives of sailors through the ages.

SAINT-JEAN-PORT-JOLI

From the maritime museum it's just 10km along Rte-132 to the small but absorbing woodcarving displays and shop at the **Musée des Anciens Canadiens ❷** (https://museedesanciens-canadiens.com; daily: mid-May to mid-July 9am–5.30pm; mid-July to Aug 8.30am–7pm; Sept to mid-Oct 9am–5pm; $8), on the edge of **Saint-Jean-Port-Joli ❸**.

The traditional Québécois folk art of woodcarving flourished in the 18th and 19th centuries, but had almost expired by the 1930s, when the three **Bourgault brothers** (Médard, Jean-Julien and André) established their workshop near here. The museum has an interesting collection of woodcarvings cut in white pine and walnut, many of which are the work of the Bourgaults. You can peruse the galleries of the most popular woodcarvers in the region along Saint-Jean-Port-Joli's long main street, a few kilometres east. Have lunch at **La Boustifaille** (see ❶).

Musée Maritime du Québec

SAINT-ROCH-DES-AULNAIES

From *La Boustifaille* drive 11km along Rte-132 to the village of **Saint-Roch-des-Aulnaies**, where a gorgeous water mill and manor house have survived at **La Seigneurie des Aulnaies ❹** (www.laseigneuriedesaulnaies.qc.ca; late June to early Sept daily 10am–5pm; $15). The Ferrée River still powers Québec's largest bucket wheel in the estate's three-storey grist mill, the Moulin Banal. The mill offers flour-grinding displays and mouthwatering options in the café. Just upstream, the veranda-wrapped Victorian manor house has period rooms, guides in costume and diverting interactive displays.

KAMOURASKA

Some 37km northeast along Rte-132, **Kamouraska ❺** is a pleasant village that boasts many examples of the Bas-Saint-Laurent region's most distinctive architectural feature, the **Kamouraska roof**. Extended to keep the rainwater off the walls, the arched and rounded eaves project from the houses in a design borrowed from the shipyards. One of the best examples is the **Villa Saint-Louis** (125 av Morel), a private residence once home to Adolphe Basile-Routhier, the man who penned the words to Canada's national anthem. The village contains an art centre, regional museum and several art galleries worth browsing, as well as excellent restaurants: have dinner at **Côté Est** (see ❷) and spend the night here (see page 111).

DAY 2: RIVIÈRE-DU-LOUP

Breakfast is always a pleasure in Kamouraska – make a stop at **Café Du Clocher** (see ❸), before driving 40km to **Rivière-du-Loup ❻**, a prosperous-looking place, whose hilly centre is complete with broad streets and handsome Victorian villas. Though the **Musée du Bas Saint-Laurent** (300 Rue Saint-Pierre; www.mbsl.qc.ca; July to mid-Sept daily 9am–5pm, check website for seasonal opening times; $7) is a good introduction to the history and culture of the area, the main reason to stop here is to take a **boat trip**; you may see beluga, minke and finback whales throughout the summer. All the companies are located by the marina at 200 Rue Hayward: try Croisières AML (www.croisieresaml.com) or La Société Duvetnor (https://duvetnor.com). There are lots of places to eat along **Rue Lafontaine** in the centre of town.

PARC NATIONAL DU BIC

Aim to spend the rest of the day in the **Parc National du Bic ❼** (sepaq.com/pq/bic; $8.90) some 90km (1hr) northeast of Rivière-du-Loup (take Autoroute-20 to save time). Encompassing the rocky wooded hummocks of the St Lawrence shoreline, it's possible to see herds of grey and harbour seals, particularly during August and September in the main sector of the park, Rivière-du-Sud-Ouest. The **Rivière-du-Sud-Ouest Visitors Centre** at the main entrance

Kamouraska landscape   *Wood sculpture of village in L'Islet*

hours vary throughout the year) provides exhibits and maps of the park.

Discovery and Visitors Centre-Rioux Farm

The **Discovery and Visitors Centre** at **Rioux Farm** in the centre of the park also offers information, a convenience store and shop. The **Chemin-du-Nord** (4km round-trip; 1hr 15min) hiking trail is a gentle stroll along the estuary shoreline from the Discovery and Visitors Centre – a highlight is the **Rose des Thés**, a teahouse in a colonial revival cottage. Three cycle paths also depart from the Discovery and Visitors Centre; the **La Coulée** (10km round-trip; 1hr 30min) provides great views of Pic Champlain and Baie des Ha! Ha! (rent bikes at the centre). At the other end of the park, shuttle buses (late June to Aug daily every 30min 12.30–2.30pm; $5.50 one way, $9.50 return) leave from the **Cap-à-l'Orignal Visitors Centre** up to **Pic Champlain**, a stunning 346m lookout in the western sector of the park.

LE BIC

It's possible to spend the night in the national park, but you'll find more comfortable lodgings (see page 111) 4km to the northeast in the village of **Le Bic** ❸. Perched on a low ridge above its snout-shaped harbour, Le Bic is a handsome medley of old and modern architecture, with good places to eat (see ❹). Classical music lovers should visit in early August for the **Concerts aux Îles du Bic** (www.bicmusique.com), a four-day outdoor chamber music festival that features performances, mostly here and in Rimouski.

DAY 3: RIMOUSKI

From Le Bic drive 16km to the university town of **Rimouski** ❾, where it's worth stopping for the **Musée Régional de Rimouski** (35 rue St-Germain Ouest; https://museerimouski.qc.ca; mid-June to early Sept daily 10am–5.30pm; early Sept to mid-June Wed–Sun noon–5pm, Thu until 7pm; $7). The museum is housed in the oldest church in Eastern Québec with an intact exterior; the three floors inside have been renovated and now focus on rotating exhibits on local history and contemporary art.

POINTE-AU-PÈRE

A few kilometres east from Rimouski along Hwy-132, the small town of **Pointe-au-Père** contains the **Site historique maritime de la Pointe-au-Père** (http://shmp.qc.ca; mid-June to mid-Sept daily 9am–6pm, check website for seasonal hours; $10.50; Onondaga June to early Oct daily 9am–6pm; $17, or $23 with museum), featuring a museum, submarine and lighthouse ($26 for all three). The **Empress of Ireland Museum**, housed in a building resembling a tilting ship, tells the story of the *Empress of Ireland*, a luxury liner

Lighthouse in Rimousk[i]

that sank offshore here in 1914 – it was a disaster second only to the *Titanic*, with more than 1,000 lives lost. In summer you can also take a self-guided tour of the **HMCS Onondaga** submarine, berthed at the nearby pier, which patrolled the North Atlantic for the Canadian navy between 1967 and 2000.

Pointe-au-Père Lighthouse National Historic Site

End your tour at the **Pointe-au-Père Lighthouse National Historic Site** ❿

(www.pc.gc.ca/fr/lhn-nhs/qc/pointe aupere; early June to early Oct daily 9am–6pm; $4; $20 with submarine; $13.50 with museum; $26 for all three), which offers fantastic views from the top of its lighthouse, the second tallest in the country (at 33m). The adjacent keeper's house contains an exhibit on the lighthouses of the St Lawrence, while the Fog Alarm Shed has a display on sound signals. From here the **Gaspé Peninsula** (see page 97) awaits, or it's a 3.5 hour drive back to Québec City.

Food and Drink

❶ LA BOUSTIFAILLE

547 av de Gaspé ouest, Saint-Jean-Port-Joli; tel: 418-598 3061; www.rocheaveillon.com; mid-May to early Oct daily 8am–9pm (closed Mon–Wed in May); $$

For gigantic portions of Québécois food – think *ragoût de boulettes* (spicy meatballs), *cipâte aux trois viands* (meat pie) and *pattes de cochon* (pig's feet stew) – head to this cheerful restaurant that shares a building with La Roche à Veillon theatre.

❷ CÔTÉ EST

76 av Morel, Kamouraska; tel: 418-308 0739; www.cote-est.ca; mid-May to early Oct Thu–Sun 11am–6pm; $$

Fresh and local food (plus local beers and ciders), including seal burgers, seaweed and shrimp pita, scallops from the Magdalen Islands, and maple donuts to finish. Check

out the view over the St Lawrence from the patio. Reservation recommended.

❸ CAFÉ DU CLOCHER

90 av Morel, Kamouraska; tel: 418-492 7365; June–Oct 8am–10pm; $

Head to this bistro (set in a 19th-century stable) to try the excellent coffee or local delicacy, smoked eel, on a bagel with cream cheese and capers as well as a range of vegetarian dishes under $20.

❹ CHEZ SAINT-PIERRE

129 rue du Mont Saint Louis, Le Bic; tel: 418-736 5051; http://chezstpierre.ca; mid-May to early Oct Thu–Sun 11am–6pm; $$

Helmed by indomitable chef Colombe St-Pierre, this gem knocks out superb dishes with local produce; incredible ratatouille, gazpacho, fresh fish, barbecued beef, locally made sausages, ceviche, pastas and more – the seasonal menus change frequently.

Perce Rock from Bonaventure Island

GASPÉ PENINSULA LOOP

The vast and isolated Gaspé Peninsula contains some of Québec's wildest national parks and most spectacular scenery, from towering waterfalls to Percé Rock, the world's most accessible northern gannet colony, and remarkable historic sites that combine Acadian, Indigenous, British and French cultures.

DISTANCE: 690km

TIME: 3 days

START: Rimouski

END: Carleton-sur-Mer

POINTS TO NOTE: This tour is designed as a road-trip, making a loop around the Gaspé Peninsula from Rimouski, where it connects with the Bas-Saint-Laurent route (see page 92). It ends at Carleton-sur-Mer, from where it's 245km (3hr) back to Rimouski. The three-day section described below begins at Parc National Forillon, some 375km (5hr) from Rimouski. Most sights on the route close partially or completely from September to May. As a major summer holiday spot, the Gaspé gets especially busy during the last two weeks of July; book accommodation and activities in advance. For accommodation options on the route see page 111. The main information centre for the Gaspésie is in Mont-Joli at 1020 blvd Jacques-Cartier (www.tourisme-gaspesie.com; Mon–Fri 8.30am–4.30pm).

Bounded by the Gulf of St Lawrence to the north and west, and by the Baie des Chaleurs to the south and east, the Gaspé Peninsula is roughly 550km long, with the Chic-Choc Mountains and rolling highlands dominating the interior and the northern shore. It has always been sparsely inhabited with limited economic opportunities, its remote communities eking out an existence from the turbulent seas and the rocky soil. But the landscape provides some truly spectacular scenery, especially in the Parc National Forillon, at the tip of the peninsula, with its mountain and coastal hikes and wonderfully rich wildlife. Just to the south of the latter, the village of Percé is famous for the offshore Rocher Percé, an extraordinary limestone monolith that has been a magnet for travellers for more than 100 years.

PARC NATIONAL FORILLON

The most enticing section of this route kicks off at the very tip of the peninsula, at the magnificent **Parc National**

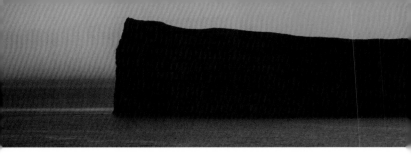

Forillon (www.pc.gc.ca/en/pn-np/qc/forillon; $7.90), encompassing thick forest and mountains, crossed by hiking trails and fringed by stark cliffs along a deeply indented coastline. The splendour of the landscape is complemented by the wildlife: black bear, moose, beaver, porcupine and red fox are all common to the area. From the coastal paths around Cap Gaspé itself, whales, such as humpback, fin and minke, and harbour porpoise can also be spotted (May–Oct). Roughly triangular in shape, the park is sandwiched between the Gulf of St Lawrence and Gaspé Bay and encircled by routes 197 and 132: the former crossing the interior to delineate the western limits of the park, the latter mostly keeping to the seashore and

threading through **L'Anse-au-Griffon** ❶ and **Cap-des-Rosiers** ❷ – tiny coastal villages with views onto the Gulf and Forillon's wooded parkland. Buy supplies at either village if you want a picnic for lunch. The park remains accessible all year round, but trails and services are not maintained between mid-October and May. To get an early start in Forillon, realistically you'll need an extra day to get to L'Anse-au-Griffon (you really need a week to cover the peninsula at a more leisurely pace).

Cap-des-Rosiers Lighthouse

Before entering the park proper on Rte-132, stop at the much-photographed **Cap-des-Rosiers Lighthouse** ❸ (www.pharecapdesrosiers.ca; site

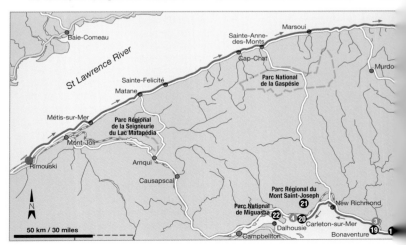

Rocher Perce

open late June to early Sept daily 8am–6pm; $3, tours $10), at 34m the tallest in Canada. Built between 1853 and 1858, it was rebuilt in marble in 1984 and has been completely automated since 1981. Guided tours of the interior (with a climb to the top for sensational views) run every 30min in summer; otherwise there's little point in paying the $3 just to enter the grounds.

Visitor Information & Discovery Centre (North Area)

The park's **Visitor Information & Discovery Centre** ❹ (June to early Sept daily 9am–5pm) opened in 2021 at the northern entrance to the park, just off Rte-132 around 4km down the road

from Cap-des-Rosiers Lighthouse. Check out the exhibits and load up on the latest trail information here, before continuing south of Rte-132. Stretch your legs at **La Chute trailhead** ❺, 4.5km further on, where a 1km trail loops through maple and cedar groves to a lacy 17-metre waterfall (there are some steep stairs here).

Grand Grave

Around 3.5km beyond the waterfall turn off Rte-132 and head into the southern sector of the park, where it's 6.6km to **Grand Grave** ❻ – if you haven't paid already there's an entrance booth along this stretch of road. You'll first pass the **Dolbel-Roberts House** (check park website for opening times) where the "Gaspesians from Land's End" exhibit sheds light on their history, including how their property was controversially expropriated to form the park 1970. A little further on, the **Hyman & Son's General Store** (late July to early Sept daily 10am–4.30pm) occupies the ground floor of the original home built by William Hyman in 1864. Half a kilometre along the road, **L'Anse-Blanchette** (check park website for opening times) comprises a fisherman's house, fish shed and various structures used by the Blanchette family to dry cod, also painstakingly restored. If you fancy a decent hike, keep going; otherwise you can return to the Hyman Store where a road leads down to the docks for **whale-watch-**

Northern Gannet pairs on Bonaventure Island

ing tours operated by **Croisière Baie de Gaspé** (www.baleines-forillon.com; July to mid-Oct).

Les Graves trail and Cap Gaspé

The best of the park's hiking trails is **Les Graves**, which you can join at **L'Anse-aux-Amérindiens** , just under 3km from L'Anse-Blanchette, at the end of the surfaced road (cars can go no further). From here it's an 8km round-trip (4hr 30min) hike to the tip of **Cap Gaspé** , otherwise known as "Land's End". The path rises and falls until it reaches the **Cape Gaspé Lighthouse**, which is set on a 95m cliff with the sea on three sides; from here you can descend down a steep path to the ocean around Land's End itself. The first lighthouse was built in 1873, but this is the third version, completed in 1950.

Fort Peninsula

From L'Anse-aux-Amérindiens it's 19km back along Rte-132 and the shore of Gaspé Bay to **Fort Peninsula** , one of the few World War II shore batteries in Canada to have been completely preserved and open to the public. It saw action between 1942 and 1944, when German U-Boats sank 23 Allied ships during the Battle of the St. Lawrence.

Penouille Visitor's Centre

Just along the road from Fort Peninsula is the national park's **Penouille Visitor's Centre** (late June to early Oct daily 9am–5pm), where the **Taïga trail** is an easy 3km loop through beautiful boreal forest to a viewpoint over the Penouille salt marsh, a favoured bird-watching spot.

GASPÉ BAY

From Penouille continue 20km to the town of Gaspé on the other side of the bay, where you can have dinner and stay the night. If there's time on route, stop at the informative **Site d'Interprétation Micmac de Gespeg** (783 blvd Pointe-Navarre; www.micmacgespeg.ca; late June to mid-Oct daily 9am–noon and 1–5pm; $11.25), which does a good job of highlighting the Indigenous Mi'kmaq culture of the Gaspé, and the adjacent **Sanctuaire Notre-Dame-de-Pointe-Navarre** , a popular church and pilgrimage site.

GASPÉ

The humdrum town and port of **Gaspé** itself straddles the hilly estuary of the York River, where the biggest attraction is the waterfront **Birthplace of Canada** (https://berceaudu canada.com). The site contains Jacques Cartier's Cross Monument (aka the **Cross of Gaspé**), a granite monolith raised in 1934 to commemorate the arrival of Cartier around here in 1534, as well as a series of recon

Percé Rock   *Fort Péninsule*

structed structures designed to replicate the village as it was in 1900. This living museum" with costumed characters opens July to early September (Mon–Sat–10am–5pm), but you can wander the site and see the cross at any time. Have dinner tonight at **Brise Bise** (see ❶).

DAY 2

Musée de la Gaspésie

Make time for the **Musée de la Gaspésie** (80 blvd Gaspé; https://museede lagaspesie.ca; daily: June to early Sept 9am–5pm; early Sept to May 11am–4pm; $20) this morning before leaving Gaspé, an excellent museum that illuminates the history but also the social issues that have confronted the inhabitants of this isolated peninsula. Outside, the **Jacques Cartier Monument** comprises six striking bronze dolmens carved in relief that record Cartier's first meeting with the St. Lawrence Iroquoians in 1534.

PERCÉ

Some 60km south from Gaspé on Rte-132 lies **Percé ⑭**, once a humble fishing community but now a booming holiday destination thanks to the adjacent national park and the gargantuan limestone rock that rears up from the sea here, facing the reddish cliffs of the shore. One of the most celebrated natural phenomena in Canada, the **Rocher-Percé ⑮** is nearly 500m long and 90m high, and is a surreal sight at dawn or sunset, when it appears bathed in an eerie golden iridescence. You can get a good view from **Cap Mont Joli** (from the parking lot at the end of Rue Mont-Joli; $1).

Parc national de l'Île-Bonaventure-et-du-Rocher-Percé

In the centre of Percé, on the waterfront, you'll find **Le Chafaud Discovery & Visitors Centre** (late May to mid-Oct daily 9am–5pm) for the **Parc national de l'Île-Bonaventure-et-du-Rocher**-Percé (www.sepaq.com/pq/bon/index.dot?language_id=1). Exhibits highlight the history, flora and fauna of the park, as well as the history of French fisherman in Percé from the 16th century. At nearby **La Neigère** on Rue du Quai, you can pay the park entry fee ($8.90) and organize cruises (from $40) around Rocher-Percé and offshore **l'Île-Bonaventure ⑯** (allowing views of the latter's famous colony of Northern Gannets); hikers will want to be let off on l'Île-Bonaventure to tackle the **four trails** (for a total of 15km) that criss-cross its wild headlands. You can pick up a later boat to get back to Percé. See Les Bateliers de Percé (www.lesbateliersdeperce.com) and Les Croisières Julien Cloutier (http://croisieres-julien-cloutier.com/web). You can eat on the island at the park managed **Le Relais des Fous** or **Resto des Margaulx**, or grab

Carleton-sur mer lighthou...

a beer and snack in Percé at **Pub Pit Caribou** (see ❷).

Mont-Sainte-Anne

One of the most spectacular longer-range views of Rocher Percé is from the top of **Mont-Sainte-Anne** ❼ (free), that rises directly behind Percé; the main path is signposted from behind the church on Rue de l'Église. The steep 3km walk takes about an hour each way. A separate trail leads off the main path to **La Grotte**, a lovely spot with waterfalls and statues of the Virgin Mary nestled into the crevasses of the mountain. About halfway up Mont-Sainte-Anne, another trail forks off to the **Plateforme Vitrée Suspendue** ($10), a spectacular glass viewing platform hanging 200m above the town. It's part of the **Percé Geopark** (www.geoparcdeperce.com), which also hosts the Tektonik multimedia show at the Pavillon Expérientiel in town. You can take a shuttle bus ($6) up or down the trail from here, and there's also a zipline. For accommodation in Percé see page 111.

DAY 3: NEW CARLISLE

Get an early start for the 115km drive southwest along Rte-132 to **New Carlisle** ❽. You're now traversing the south shore of the peninsula along the **Baie des Chaleurs** that separates the Gaspé from New Brunswick. The small bilingual settlement of New Carlisle is best known as th childhood home of **René Lévesque** (1922–1987), ex-premier of Québec founder of the Parti Québécois i 1968 and all-round local hero. Yo could happily spend half a day here visiting the **Espace René-Lévesque** (120 blvd Gérard D Lévesque; http:/ espacerenelevesque.com; June–Sep daily 9am–6pm; $12), a stylish trib ute to the Québécois political gian and the **Kempffer Cultural and Inte pretation Center** (125 blvd Gérar D Lévesque; late June–Aug dail 9am–5pm; $10), which chronicles th history of the town in a grand Victoria pile built in 1868 by local business man Robert Kempffer. Just outside New Carlisle there's also the **Site His torique du Banc-De-Paspébiac** (www shbp.ca; early June to early Oct dail 9am–5pm; $15), a preserved cod fish ing station and shipyard dating back t the early 19th century.

BONAVENTURE

Aim to have lunch with a sea view further 15km along Rte-132 at th cute, folksy-styled **Café Acadien** (se ❸), in **Bonaventure** ❾. The town wa founded by Acadian refugees nea the mouth of the Bonaventure Rive in 1760, one of the stories told a the enlightening **Musée Acadien d Québec** (95 av Port-Royal; https:/ museeacadien.com; see website fo opening hours; $13).

Forillon National Park scenic road

CARLETON-SUR-MER

End this three-day tour at **Carleton-sur-Mer** ⑳, another 70km along the Baie des Chaleurs from Bonaventure. It's a pleasant spot to spend the night, but before you leave make sure you visit **Mont Saint-Joseph** ㉑ (https://mont saintjoseph.com; $8.50), which looms high above the town.

You can drive to the 555-metre summit, but the walk up is much more rewarding. Whichever way you choose, it's presided over by the **Oratoire Notre-Dame-du-Mont-Saint-Joseph**, a church that incorporates the walls of a stone chapel built on the site in 1935.

There's also the fascinating **Parc national de Miguasha** ㉒ (www.sepaq. com/pq/mig/index.dot; $8.90) some 20km to the west of Carleton off Hwy-132, famous for its fossils. After stretching your legs, Carlton boasts some surprisingly good places to eat and drink – try **Microbrasserie Le Naufrageur** (see ④). For accommodation see page 111.

Food and Drink

① BRISE-BISE

135 rue de la Reine, Gaspé; tel: 418-368 1456; https://brisebise.ca; daily 11am–midnight; $$

A great bistro and a swinging bar at night, with terraces on each of its two floors and serving a variety of dishes, from poké bowls to roast beef.

② PUB PIT CARIBOU

182 Hwy-132, Percé; tel: 418-782 1443; https://pitcaribou.com; daily noon–3am (seasonal hours); $$

Set inside a historic white-tiled building, this popular microbrewery oozes a relaxed charm and serves its locally brewed beers on tap, of which the blonde and IPA are standouts. They serve snacks, but they also allow you bring in your own food.

③ CAFÉ ACADIEN

168 rue de Beaubassin, Bonaventure; tel: 418-534 4276; www.cafeacadien. com; June–Sept Wed–Sun 8am–3pm and 5–9pm; $$

This cute café right on the water, decorated in a simple but folksy style, serves imaginative Acadian and French dishes, from salted catfish fishcakes to *bouillabaisse gaspésienne*.

④ MICROBRASSERIE LE NAUFRAGEUR

586 blvd Perron, Carleton; tel: 418-534 4276; www.lenaufrageur.com; June–Sept daily 11.30am–11pm; $$

Poutines, burgers, pizza, tapas, sandwiches, soups and salads are served at this cozy restaurant and microbrewery to accompany their excellent craft beers – specialties include beers flavoured with raspberries, espresso coffee and teas.

DIRECTORY

Hand-picked hotels and restaurants to suit all budgets and tastes, organised by area, plus select nightlife listings and an overview of the best books and films to give you a flavour of the region.

ACCOMMODATION

Whilst the major cities and tourist areas of Québec offer plenty of accommodation, choices can dwindle dramatically when travelling through the more rural regions of the province, especially in the far north – best to book all accommodation as far in advance as possible. In general, chain motels are far scarcer than in provinces further west. Hotels and even motels tend to be on the pricey side in the peak summer months, and many hotels and B&Bs close completely for the coldest half of the year. Camping is popular in national parks in the summer, and there are a handful of hostels in the bigger cities, but true budget options are rare throughout the province. Note also that total sales tax (GST + QST) is high here.

On the plus side are family-owned hotels, gîtes and B&Bs offering exceptional friendly service and home-cooked meals, often housed in historic 19th-century properties with a ton of character.

Local tourist information offices will invariably help out with accommodation if you get stuck: most offer free advice and will book a place free of charge.

Price for a standard double room for one night in high season:
$ = below $100
$$ = $100–150
$$$ = $151–200
$$$$ = above $200

Montréal

Auberge Alternative
358 rue St-Pierre; tel: 514-282 8069, www.auberge-alternative.qc.ca; $
This comfortable, arty hostel is in a refurbished 1875 Vieux-Montréal warehouse and has a range of dorms, and private rooms. The hostel celebrates the local art community, with a small gallery showcasing emerging artists. They also offer bike and camping equipment rental.

Hôtel Bonaparte
447 rue St-François-Xavier; tel: 514-844 1448, http://bonaparte.com; $$$
Sleep amid history at this handsome inn, steps from the Basilique Notre Dame, which was built in 1886 and is shaded by smart burgundy awnings. Inside, the quarters are decked out with wrought-iron headboards, hardwood floors and French dormer windows; some have views of the Basilique's gardens. Breakfast included.

Auberge les Bons Matins
1401 av Argyle; tel: 514-931 9167, www.bonsmatins.com; $$
On a tree-lined street near downtown and busy rue Crescent, this well-appointed B&B-style inn has spacious rooms and suites, each with special architectural features (archways, exposed brick, wood beams, fireplace) and large windows.

Fairmont Le Chateau Frontenac Hotel Québec City

Le Petit Hôtel

168 rue St-Paul ouest; tel: 514-940 0360, https://petithotelmontreal.com; $$$

Bright orange accents play against old stone at this whimsical Vieux-Montréal hotel, housed in an elegant 19th-century building. Stylish rooms come in clothing sizes – S, M, L, XL; the lobby café serves up ink-black espressos and robust red wines; and the glass front doors swing open onto the cobblestone streets of the old town. Bicycles available for guests' use.

Le Saint-Sulpice Hôtel

414 rue St-Sulpice; tel: 514-288 1000, www.lesaintsulpice.com; $$$

It would be hard to find a better-placed hotel in Vieux-Montréal, in the shadow of the Basilique Notre-Dame. The hotel is all suites, each with a fireplace and kitchenette, and some with an ample terrace. Restaurant Oskar serves food made with locally-inspired ingredients, in a leafy courtyard overlooking the neighbouring Sulpician seminary gardens.

The Laurentians

Le Chalet Beaumont

1451 rue Beaumont, Val-David; tel: 819-322 1972, www.chaletbeaumont.com; $

This massive chalet serves as Val-David's hostel, with both dorm and private rooms. Curl up by the fire in the winter and enjoy great outdoor views. They can also arrange for outdoor activities.

La Maison de Bavière

1470 chemin de la Rivière, Val-David; tel: 819-322 3528, www.maisondebaviere.com. $$$

You can watch the river rapids from the fireplace-warmed sitting room in the winter or sit outside on the terrace and sip away on a glass of wine in the summer at this pleasant, small, Bavarian-themed B&B. It also has two studio apartments, with kitchen, for those interested in longer stays.

Manitonga Hostel

2213 chemin du Village, old village of Mont-Tremblant; tel: 819-425 6008, https://manitongahostel.com. $

An excellently kitted out hostel, with a café and bar, swimming in the lake behind the hostel, free canoe rental and organized treks and ski packages.

Hôtel Quintessence

3004 chemin de la Chapelle, Mont-Tremblant; tel: 819-425 3400, www.hotelquintessence.com. $$$$

Nature and nurture come together splendidly in this all-suite boutique hotel: nature with the views of the glistening Lac Tremblant; nurture from the concierge who can arrange for ski lessons or personally deliver wood for your in-room fireplace, and from the heated marble floors in the bathroom. You can indulge in further pampering at the Spa Sans Sabots or at the inviting wine bar. Whatever you choose to do, this is a great place to stay.

Manoir Hovey Treetops Pines Suite

Cantons-de-l'Est and the Route des Vins

Gîte Au Chant de l'Onde
6 Rue de l'Église, Frelighsburg; tel: 450-298 5676, www.auchantdelonde.ca; $$
Fabulous B&B overlooking the Aux Brochets River, with three air-conditioned rooms decked out in eclectic Mesoamerican, Lapland and North African styles respectively, and organic breakfasts made with local garden produce.

Manoir Hovey
575 chemin Hovey, North Hatley; tel: 819-842 2421, www.manoirhovey.com; $$$
This classy 19th-century colonnaded inn sits in sloping grounds on the banks of Lake Massawippi and offers a variety of outdoor activities, from kayaking to windsurfing. Plush alpine rooms feature four-poster beds. You can dine on market-fresh Québécois and French cuisine at Le Hatley restaurant.

Auberge Marquis de Montcalm
797 rue du Général-De Montcalm, Sherbrooke; tel: 819-823 7773, www.marquisdemontcalm.ca. $$
This lovely B&B near the Magog River gorge features comfortable rooms, hardwood floors and goose-down comforters. A robust breakfast – from fresh fruits to vegetable quiche to scrambled eggs with sundried tomatoes – is included.

Vignoble Bromont
1095 chemin Nord, Brigham; tel: 450-263 4988, https://vignoblebromont.ca; $$
This winery offers simple but cosy and well-maintained a/c rooms close to the vineyards, with access to shared kitchen, dining room and lounge with piano.

The Centre

Manoir De Blois
197 rue Bonaventure, Trois-Rivières; tel: 819-373 1090, https://manoirdeblois.com; $$
Relax in the elegant rooms of this 1828 stone house with original wood floors and an antique-strewn salon. The family-run inn also serves a filling breakfast

Québec City

Hôtel Le Château de Pierre
17 av Ste-Geneviève; tel: 418-694 0429, https://chateaudepierre.com; $$$
A lavish 1853 English colonial-style mansion with 15 plush rooms; all are en suite and those without a/c have balconies. It once served as the Consulate of the Republic of Argentina, becoming a hotel in 1960.

Auberge International de Québec
19 rue Ste-Ursule; tel: 418-694 0755, https://en.hiquebec.ca; $
This 300-bed HI hostel, in a former 1790s hospice run by nuns, is often full and can be impersonal, though it offers dorm beds and private rooms, a café Bistro, free breakfast, free Wi-Fi, laundry facilities, luggage lockers, kitchens and a bar.

Hôtel Maison du Fort
21 av Ste-Geneviève; tel: 418-692 4375, www.hotelmaisondufort.com; $$

Charming hotel built in Georgian style by architect Charles Baillargé and completed in 1851, with 11 impeccably designed, spacious rooms. Theres also a two-room apartment with kitchenette.

Maison Historique James Thompson

47 rue Ste-Ursule; tel: 418-694 9042, http://bedandbreakfastquebec.com; $$

A B&B in a historic house with sleigh beds, antiques throughout, a lovely sitting room and filling breakfasts. James Thompson, a fortification expert with the British Army and a veteran of the Battle of the Plains of Abraham, constructed the house in 1793.

Auberge St-Antoine

8 rue St-Antoine; tel; 418-692 2211, www.saint-antoine.com; $$$$

Contemporary hotel divided into two buildings next to the Musée de la Civilisation; Québec City's only remaining early-19th century dockside warehouse, and six historically-themed suites in the 18th-century James Hunt House. All rooms are exceedingly spacious, tastefully decorated (some with a historic theme) and several have views of the river. Massage therapy, a private cinema, gym, babysitters and indoor valet parking are among the top-notch services.

Côte-de-Beaupré and Charlevoix

Auberge des 3 Canards

115 côte Bellevue, La Malbaie; tel: 418-665 3761, www.auberge3canards.com/en; $$

Graceful inn with 48 comfortable rooms – most have their own private balcony overlooking the river – and one of the area's finest restaurants.

Hôtel Fairmont Le Manoir Richelieu

181 rue Richelieu, La Malbaie; tel: 418-665 3703, www.fairmont.com; $$$$

A luxurious and historic château replete with a golf course, spa with indoor and outdoor pools, a handful of restaurants and bars, and a full range of high-end amenities. Most of the 405 rooms have spectacular views over the St Lawrence.

Auberge La Muse

39 rue Saint Jean Baptiste, Baie-Saint-Paul; tel: 418-435 6839, www.lamuse.com; $$

Right in the centre of town, this beautiful Victorian-era inn has twelve large, prettily decorated rooms – including an "energizing suite". Facilities include a restaurant, health centre and gift shop selling food made on-site.

Maison Otis

23 rue St-Jean-Baptiste, Baie-Saint-Paul; tel: 418-435 2255, https://maisonotis.com; $$$

One of the best hotels in town, with a pleasant, country-house feel (the property dates back to 1836). The 20 rooms and five suites (some with exposed beams) have been completely renovated; some have jacuzzis and fireplaces. There's also an on-site restaurant and bar.

Saguenay Loop

Baie-Éternité Campground
Rivière-Éternité; tel: 418-272 1556,
www.sepaq.com; $
The Baie-Éternité sector's main campground is located right on the bay; as well as campsites, there are ready-to-camp tents and five new Écho cabins (with kitchens and two rooms for four persons). Blackflies love this area, though the worst is over by late July; dress appropriately and bring repellent.

Chalet les Berges
945 Chemin Des Berges, Alma; tel: 418-693 6059, https://chaletlesberges.com; $$
B&B in a beautiful cottage, with stellar views of the Saguenay River and three comfy and air-conditioned rooms, 10min from Alma centre. There's a lovely outdoor terrace, Jacuzzi and private beach.

Maison Hovington
285 rue des Pionniers, Tadoussac; tel: 418-235 4466, www.maisonhovington.com; $$
B&B in a charming 1895 house, with five aging but comfy rooms and fabulous views over the bay. Excellent home-cooked breakfasts. Open May–Oct.

Hôtel Tadoussac
165 rue du Bord-de-l'Eau, Tadoussac; tel: 418-235 4421, www.hoteltadoussac.com; $$$
This rambling red-roofed hotel, established back in 1864, is the pick of Tadoussac's accommodation options, with surcharged river-view rooms, refined restaurants, swimming pool, miniature golf and tennis courts.

Côte-Nord

Château Arnaud
403 av Arnaud, Sept-Îles; tel: 855-960 5511, https://chateauarnaud.com; $$
Plush, modern accommodation right on the marina, with spectacular views of the islands and stylish rooms, some with kitchenettes, gym and spa treatments available.

Auberge la Cache
183 chemin d'en Haut, Natashquan; tel: 418-726 3347, www.aubergelacache.com; $$$
The 10-room Auberge la Cache is pleasantly furnished and a nice enough place to stay, though it's a little pricey. Its restaurant is open June to early Sept.

Auberge Internationale Le Tangon
555 av Cartier, Sept-Îles; tel: 418-962 8180 www.aubergeletangon.com; $
Friendly hostel two blocks from the waterfront, set inside a 1930s clapboard schoolhouse (which makes it a historic building up here). Features three dorms and 13 private rooms with shared bathrooms, bright shared kitchen and lounge plus a tranquil courtyard outside.

Hôtel Le Manoir
8 av Cabot, Baie-Comeau; tel: 418-296 3391, https://manoirbc.com; $$
A historic former manor, this rambling stone hotel overlooks the St Lawrence River and offers a variety of handsome

Auberge Saint–Antoine Luxe Terrasse Foyer King

rooms. Bikes are available for rent and there's a fitness room and tennis court. The on-site restaurant Bistro la Marée Haute serves excellent seafood dishes.

Bas-Saint-Laurent

Auberge du Mange Grenouille
148 rue de Sainte-Cécile-du-Bic, Le Bic; tel: 418-736 5656; $$
Graceful inn with attractively furnished double rooms and a superb restaurant with a decidedly upscale and expensive table d'hôte. Open May to mid-Oct.

La Maison aux Coquillages
168 av Morel, Kamouraska; tel: 418-308 1844, www.lamaisonauxcoquillages.com; $$$$
The bright yellow "Shell House" is one of the village's best B&Bs; all rooms have private bathrooms and balconies with views of the river. Comes with terrace, solarium and full breakfast.

Motel Cap Blanc
300 av Morel, Kamouraska; tel: 418-492 2919, www.motelcapblanc.com; $$
A simple motel with river views and tall windows in the 11 rooms (all with a private terrace and a kitchenette). Open May–Nov.

Hotel Rimouski
225 blvd René-Lepage Est, Rimouski; tel: 418-725 5000, https://hotelrimouski.com; $$
The Rimouski has comfortable rooms and suites; and a health centre, pool and bikes available for guest use. The loca-tion is central and the sunset views from the rooms are not to be missed.

Gaspé Peninsula

La Maison Rouge
125 Rte-132, Percé; tel: 418-782 2227, www.lamaisonrouge.ca; $
A dynamic hostel that rents kayaks and runs excursions to l'Île-Bonaventure. Dorm beds are in a renovated barn, while simple but adequate double rooms are in the main building.

Manoir Belle Plage
474 blvd Perron, Carleton; tel: 418-364 3388, https://manoirbelleplage.com; $$
A large, pretty, yellow inn with a touch of class, a wide range of amenities and a range of supremely comfortable rooms. Le Courlieu, the inn's maritime-themed restaurant, serves grilled seafood dishes.

Hôtel La Normandie
221 Rte-132, Percé; tel: 418-782 2112, www.normandieperce.com; $$
There's been a hotel on this site since 1937. Its cliff-top location offers superb views of the bay and that rock. Thir-ty-seven of the 45 modern rooms have balconies.

Hôtel Plante
137 rue Jacques-Cartier, Gaspé; tel: 418-368 2254, www.hotelplante.com; $$
One of the better-value motels in town, this modern place has sweeping bay views and neat, contemporary style dou-bles or two-storey suites with a kitchen.

Au Pied de Cochon chef

RESTAURANTS

In Montréal and Québec City there's a plethora of international and speciality restaurants. Montréal is a globally renowned centre of food culture, with everything from high-end French food to its own style of bagels. Beyond these cities, choices narrow dramatically; many small towns featuring just a handful of family-run cafés and bistros.

Basic dishes – poutine, burgers, pasta – are served in most places, but where the region excels is French-inspired cuisine and fresh seafood. Even in small towns you'll usually find a French-style bistro, café, or local place serving French crêpes and ice cream.

The wineries of the Cantons-de-l'Est often serve snacks, charcuterie and cheese plates with tastings. Craft breweries (or "microbrasseries") often serve decent food along with the local ales. Few restaurants in rural areas open year-round (unless there is skiing); most fully open May or June through to September or October, then close or open with limited hours thereafter.

Throughout this book, price guide for a two-course meal for one with an alcoholic drink:
$$$$ = over $75
$$$ = $51–75
$$ = $25–50
$ = below $25

Montréal

Au Pied de Cochon
536 av Duluth est; tel: 514-281 1114, https://aupieddecochon.ca; Wed–Sun 5pm–midnight; $$
Chef Martin Picard famously added foie gras to poutine. Since then, he has continued to challenge the norm, with a robustly meat-centric menu, foie gras served a dozen different ways and stuffed pig's feet (*pieds de cochon*).

La Banquise
994 rue Rachel Est, Plateau Mont-Royal; http://labanquise.com; daily 24hr; $
This shrine to poutine was opened by local fireman Pierre Barsalou in 1968. Poutine first graced the menu in the early 1980s and there are now thirty different varieties – from classic poutine to La Hot-Dog to La Reggae (with ground beef, guacamole, diced tomatoes and hot peppers).

Beautys
93 av du Mont-Royal ouest; tel: 514-849 8883, https://beautys.ca; Mon–Fri 7am–3pm, Sat–Sun 8am–4pm; $
A beloved diner with wonderful 1950s decor – and delicious breakfasts, including the dizzyingly rich Mish-Mashan omelette studded with salami and hot dog. You should also try the Beautys Bonjoura bagel heaped with egg, bacon and Cheddar cheese. Get

Au Pied de Cochon dishes   *Au Pied de Cochon dishes*

up early at the weekend to avoid the queue.

Bouillon Bilk

1595 blvd St-Laurent; tel: 514-845 1595, www.bouillonbilk.com; Mon–Fri 11.30am–2.30pm and 5.30–11pm, Sat and Sun 5.30–11pm; $$$$

The eclectic French-inspired cuisine includes guinea fowl with pistachios and duck with celery root and hazelnuts. The minimalist setting is a quiet contrast to the creativity bursting from the plates.

Club Chasse et Pêche

423 rue St-Claude; tel: 514-861 1112, www.leclubchasseetpeche.com; Tue–Sat 6–10.30pm; $$$

One of Canada's top restaurants, it has a seasonally changing menu that may include venison with polenta and aged Cheddar and rabbit ravioli. The setting is includes leather chairs, dark wood and animal-inspired lighting.

Garde Manger

408 rue St-Francois-Xavier; tel: 514-678 5044, www.gardemanger.ca; Tue–Sun 5:30–11.30pm; $$

A festive, familial atmosphere fills this popular restaurant helmed by celebrity chef Chuck Hughes. Seafood is the speciality, but equal care is given to the braised short ribs. Lively tunes, a bustling bar and a cocktail-fuelled crowd make for one of the more vibrant dining spots in Vieux-Montréal.

Schwartz's

3895 blvd St-Laurent tel: 514-842 4813, https://schwartzsdeli.com; Mon and Thu–Sun 8am–12.30am, Fri 8am–1.30am, Sat 8am–2.30am; $

A Montréal institution: a small, narrow deli serving up colossal smoked-meat sandwiches, with sometimes surly service thrown in as part of the package. Line up out the door at weekends.

Vin Mon Lapin

150 rue Saint-Zoutique est; tel: 514-379 4550; http://vinmonlapin.com; Tue–Sat 5pm–midnight; $$

In 2018, this vivacious wine bar opened, unveiling innovative small plates that live up to the famous Joe Beef culinary creativity. The ever-changing seasonal menu might include fried oysters, snails with salami and, of course, lapin (rabbit).

The Laurentians

Au Petit Poucet

1030 Rte-117, Val-David; tel: 819-322 2246, https://aupetitpoucet.ca; daily 6.30am–4pm; $$

Fill up on home-made Québécois cuisine at this longtime favourite, from smoked ham to tourtière (a minced pork pie) to baked beans.

Microbrasserie La Diable

117 chemin Kandahar, Mont-Tremblant; tel: 819-681 4546, microladiable.com; daily 11.30am–2am; $$

After a long day of skiing (or hiking), kick back at this comfortable brewpub,

Le Cellier du Roi dishes

where you can guzzle everything from black stout to Belgian wheat beer. It also serves hearty grub, like burgers, chunky chili, barbecue ribs and hot soups.

La Savoie
117 chemin Kandahar, Mont-Tremblant; tel: 819-681 4573, https://restaurantlasavoie.com; daily 5–10pm; $$$
There's nothing like fondue when you're in the mountains. This inviting Swiss chalet restaurant serves rich cheese fondue and raclette, as well as a robust wine list.

Cantons de l'Est and the Route des Vins

Auguste
82 rue Wellington Nord, Sherbrooke; tel: 819-565 9559, www.auguste-restaurant.com; Tue–Wed 11.30–2.30 & 5–10pm, Thu–Fri 11.30am–2.30pm and 5pm–11pm, Sat 10.30am–2.30pm and 5–11pm, Sun 10.30am–2.30pm and 5–10pm; $$$
Innovative, farm-to-fork Québécois cuisine, including sweet potato ravioli, black sausage served with red cabbage, and other superb grilled meats and fish.

Le Cellier du Roi
(Le Royal Bromont), 400 chemin Compton; tel: 450-534 4653, www.royalbromont.com; Wed–Fri 11.30am–9pm, Sat 5–9pm; $$$$
Set amid the landscaped grounds of Le Royal Bromont, a public golf course, the menu here is deeply rooted in the surrounding region, highlighting everything from local cheeses to home-grown gar-

den vegetables. The prix fixe dinner menu includes dishes like foie gras with smoked bison and sea bream with carrots and gingerbread.

La Table du Chef
11 rue Victoria, Sherbrooke; tel: 819-562 2258, https://latableduchef.ca; Tue–Fri 11.30am–2pm and 5.30–9pm, Sat 5.30–9pm; $$
Helmed by renowned chef Alain Labrie, this elegant restaurant excels at French-accented regional cuisine, including grilled bison with creamy polenta and elk tartare with chipotle peppers.

Québec City

Buffet de l'Antiquaire
95 rue St-Paul; tel: 418-692 2661, https://le buffetdelantiquaire.com; daily 6am–10pm; $
An old-school diner with cosy tables and bar stools, popular with locals for breakfast plus home-cooked comfort food like poutine and l'assiette Québécoise (meat pie with beans).

Café Au Bonnet d'Âne
298 rue St-Jean; tel: 418-647 3031, http://new.aubonnetdane.com; Apr–Oct daily 8am–11pm; Nov–Mar Mon–Wed and Sun 8am–10pm, Thu–Sat 8am–11pm; $
While away a few hours at this hip café bar, where you can enjoy omelettes, burgers and enormous salads at the quieter end of rue St-Jean.

Chez Jules
24 rue Ste-Anne; tel: 418-694 7000,

Le Cellier du Roi interior　　　　　　　　　　*Le Cellier du Roi dishes*

https://chezjules.ca; Mon–Fri 7.30am–
10pm, 11.30am–1.30pm and 5.30–10pm;
Sat–Sun 7.30am–10pm and 5.30–10pm; $$
The superb menu includes exquisitely
prepared items such as sole fillet with
rice, a sumptuous croque-madame and
duck foie gras. Not a place to skip des-
sert, particularly the heavenly crème
brûlée.

Chez Temporel

25 rue Couillard tel: 418-694 1813,
www.facebook.com/cheztemporel; daily
11am–8.30pm (closed Jan); $
This cosy café, near the Auberge de la
Paix hostel, offers bowls of steaming
café au lait, croissants and chocolatines,
but is also a perfect place for soups and
sandwiches.

Le Lapin Sauté

52 rue du Petit-Champlain tel: 418-692
5325, www.lapinsaute.com; Mon–Thu
11am–10pm, Fri 11am–10.30pm, Sat
9am–10.30pm, Sun 9am–10pm; $$
Very popular, reasonably priced infor-
mal bistro specializing in rabbit – even
on the breakfast menu. Dinner mains
include a rabbit poutine and an excellent cassoulet with rabbit confit and
duck sausage.

Île d'Orléans

La Goéliche

2 rue du Quai, Sainte-Pétronille; tel: 418-
828 2248, www.goeliche.ca; Mon, Wed,
Thu 8.30am–7.30pm, Tue 8.30am–2.30pm,
Fri–Sat 8.30am–8.30pm; (hours change

seasonally); $$$
This historic inn right on the water
serves dishes such as pork fillet with a
strawberry and honey sauce and salmon
steak marinated in crème de cassis.

Côte-de-Beaupré and Charlevoix

Le Café des Artistes

25 rue St-Jean-Baptiste, Baie-Saint-Paul;
tel: 418-435 5585, www.lecafedesartistes.
com; Mon–Thu 10.30am–10pm, Fri
10.30am–11pm, Sat 10am–11pm, Sun
10am–10pm; $
Popular bistro that serves desserts,
coffees and thin-crust pizzas, and fre-
quently hosts art openings. Its adjoining
club is the place to go to catch live local
and regional acts.

Maison du Bootlegger

110 Rang du Ruisseau des Frênes, just off
Rte-138 (14km north of Malbaie); tel: 418-
439 3711, www.maisondubootlegger.com;
July–Sept daily 10am–11.30pm, June and
Sept Sat–Sun 10am–11.30pm; $$
For pub food head to this fun steak-
house and hopping bar with frequent live
music. The table d'hôte includes a quirky
tour (nightly in summer) of some of the
house's rooms, connected by a warren
of passageways added when alcohol was
forbidden by the Church (guided tours
otherwise $10).

Saguenay Loop

Bistro L'Anse

319 rue St-Jean-Baptiste, L'Anse-

Cafe Boheme summer garden

Saint-Jean; tel: 418-272 4222,
www.bistrodelanse.com; Mid-May to mid-
Oct generally 11am–2pm and 5–9pm; $
At this excellent cultural and culinary
repository you can grab a seat on a terrace overlooking the fjord and munch on
dishes such as poutine, fish and chips,
and shrimp risotto, as well as salads and
burgers, and wash it all down with one of
the regional beers on tap.

Café Bohéme

239 rue des Pionniers, Tadoussac; tel: 418-
235 1180, www.lecafeboheme.com; daily:
May–June and Sept–Oct 8am–10pm; July
and Aug 7am–11pm; $$
Charming café and bistro that serves
breakfast items, fresh salads and inven-
tive dinners using local ingredients.

Chez Mathilde

227 rue des Pionniers, Tadoussac; tel: 418-
235 4443, https://chezmathildebistro.com;
June–Oct daily noon–3pm and 6–11pm;
$$$
This hip restaurant specializes in fresh
local seafood. The prices are more than
in most places in town, but a meal here
is well worth it.

Côte-Nord

La Promenade

1197 Promenade des Anciens, Havre-
Saint-Pierre; tel: 418-538 1720; daily
11am–11pm; $
Friendly seaside restaurant serving
hearty meals for lunch and dinner with a
view of the Mingan Archipelago.

Pub St-Marc

588 av Brochu, Sept-Îles; tel: 418-962
7770; Mon–Fri 11.30am–11pm, Sat–Sun
4pm–3am; $
A surprisingly stylish bar serving micro-
brews, with a more expensive restaurant
upstairs where there's great pasta and a
vast selection of salads, all under $20.

Bas-Saint-Laurent

La Belle Excuse

138 rue Notre-Dame ouest, Trois-Pistoles;
tel: 418-857 3000; June–Sept Wed–Sat
5–9pm, Sun 10am–9pm; $$
Cosy restaurant in a pretty red house
serving exceptional regional cuisine
such as smoked fish. The Sunday brunch
is a steal and there's terrace seating.

La Boustifaille

547 av de Gaspé, Saint-Jean-Port-Joli;
tel: 418-598 3061, www.rocheaveillon.
com; Mid-May to early Oct daily 8am–9pm
(closed Mon–Wed in May); $
For gigantic portions of Québécois food
(*planches à partager* to share; *menu de
jour*), head to this cheerful restaurant
that shares a building with La Roche à
Veillon theatre on the east side of town.

Café du Clocher

90 av Morel, Kamouraska; tel: 418-492
7365, http://cafeduclocher.com; June–Oct
8am–10pm; $
Head to this bistro (set in a 19th-century
stable) to try the excellent coffee. Also
don't miss their local delicacy, smoked
eel, on a bagel with cream cheese and

Cafe Boheeme

apers, as well as a range of vegetarian
ishes under $20.

'Estaminet
99 rue Lafontaine, Rivière-du-Loup; tel:
18-867 4517, www.restopubestaminet.
om; Mon–Wed 7am–11pm, Thu 7am–
nidnight, Fri 7am–1am, Sat 8am–1am, Sun
am–11pm; $$
 bustling bar near the centre, with 150
ypes of beer and fine pub food, including
noules frites.

e Saint-Patrice
69 rue Fraser, Rivière-du-Loup; tel: 418-
62 9895, www.lesaintpatrice.ca; Mon–Fri
1.30am–2pm and 5–9pm, Sat 5–9.30pm,
un 5–8pm; $$
tylish restaurant devoted to serving
xpertly prepared and arranged regional
ishes, such as smoked fish, lamb and
hellfish. It's also earned a reputation for
s thin-crust pizza, with options such as
moked salmon.

a Réserve Bistro
50 av de la Cathédrale, Rimouski; tel:
18-730 6525, www.bistrolareserve.com;
ue–Fri 11am–10pm, Sat 5–10pm; $$$
own the block from the city's cathedral,
a Réserve Bistro is one of the area's
nmistakeable and unmissable culinary
eats. The menu features inventive and
eautifully arranged meals, such as beef
houlder braised in an oatmeal stout
nd salmon tartare. Desserts such as
rème brûlée and chocolate tart are well
orth it, too.

Gaspé Peninsula

Boulangerie Le Fournand
194 Rte-132, Percé; tel: 418-782 2211,
www.boulangerielefournand.com; May–Oct
Mon–Sat 7am–2pm; $
Very much a quintessential French bak-
ery and an essential morning stop, cheery
and bustling Le Fournand tempts with
a wide assortment of brownies, loaves,
cakes, croissants and tarts. It also serves
tasty soups, sandwiches and quiches.

Café des Artistes
101 rue de la Reine, Gaspé; tel: 418-368
2255, https://cafedesartistes.co; Mon–Fri
7am-10.30pm Sat–Sun 8am–10.30pm; $
A great spot for a morning bagel and cof-
fee as well as a variety of sandwiches and
pasta.

La Maison du Pêcheur
157 Rte-132, Percé; tel: 418-782 5331,
www.maisondupecheur.ca; late May to late
Oct daily noon–10pm; $$
Top-notch seafood restaurant with pleas-
ant decor and locally-sourced produce,
with most mains, such as boiled lobster,
filet mignon, seafood chowder and seared
scallops. Reservations recommended.

La Mie Véritable
578 blvd Perron, Carleton; tel: 418-
364 6662; Mon–Sat 7am–5.30pm, Sun
8am–2pm.
An excellent bakery that uses organic
ingredients and serves coffee at its
café upstairs, La Mie d'en Haut. It's well
worth a visit if time permits.

NIGHTLIFE

Nightlife in Montréal is some of the most vibrant in North America, with a range of hopping nightclubs, to sophisticated cocktail lounges and craft beer joints. Live music and live theatre thrive in the city – this is the home of Cirque du Soleil – and there's a huge roster of local talent, from traditional chanson and folk, to heavy rock, electronica and hip hop. Québec City doesn't have quite the same line up but there are plenty of bars and live venues here too. Elsewhere, the province's burgeoning craft beer scene provides a focus for many small towns, where live music tends towards traditional folk. Festivals are a big deal here too, with even the smallest communities hosting live performances and events in the summer. The following listings are just a selection.

BARS AND TAPROOMS

Montréal
Atwater Cocktail Club
512 av Atwater; tel: 438-387 4252, www.atwatercocktailclub.com.
Scoot up to the elegant marble bar and indulge in inventive cocktails at this low-lit place in St-Henri. The changing drinks list incorporates seasonal flavours; try Patagonia Secret, made with ginger beer, Luxardo Fernet, lime and maté.

Bar Henrietta
115 av Laurier ouest; tel: 514-276 4282, http://barhenrietta.com

Kick off the night at this spirited, low-lit Portuguese tavern, filled with lots of dark and amber woods, a top-notch menu of Mediterranean wine and cava and colourful cocktails. The bonus is a tasty array of small plates, which are perfect for soaking up the alcohol.

Bily Kun
354 av du Mont-Royal est; tel: 514-845 5392, www.bilykun.com
Youthful, packed brasserie-pub, with stuffed ostrich heads overlooking tables and booths. A great world beer selection, plus DJs and occasional live bands, from jazz to funk to classical quartets.

Brutopia
1219 rue Crescent; tel: 514-393 9277, www.brutopia.net
This welcoming pub is spread over three floors, with a terrace and balcony. Exotic beers – from chocolate stout to honey wheat – are brewed on-site in the copper drums behind the bar. Live bands most nights as well as lively open-mic nights and happy hour trivia.

Coldroom
155 Saint-Paul est; tel: 514-294 6911, www.thecoldroommtl.com.
This smooth cocktail bar lives inside former industrial coldroom from 1877. Cozy up on the leather sofas, surrounded by brick walls and gilded mi

A selection of cocktails

ors, and sample your way through the inventive cocktails, such as Duck, made with dark rum, amaretto, angostura bitters and duck fat.

Isle de Garde
1039 rue Beaubien est; tel: 514-831 0181, www.isledegarde.com
This cosy bar pours a wonderful array of suds, from Berliner Melon Weisse (from Dunham, Québec) to dry, tart ciders to the house-made Isle de Garde Brown Porter Ale.

La Distillerie 1
300 rue Ontario est; tel: 514-288 7915, www.pubdistillerie.com.
Drink innovative cocktails – many made with seasonal ingredients – from mason jars at this trendy but welcoming bar. Get here early – or be prepared to wait in line.

Rest of the Quebec
À l'abri de la Tempête
286 chemin Coulombe, L'Étang-du-Nord, Îles-de-la-Madeleine; tel: 418-986 5005, https://alabridelatempete.com.
Housed in an old fish factory just short of the Dune de l'Ouest and well worth a detour, this fantastic microbrewery serves several award-winning beers made from ingredients grown on the islands.

La Barberie
310 rue St-Roch, Québec City; tel: 418-522 4373, www.labarberie.com.
Inviting microbrewery in Saint-Roch with a small selection of stand-out ales.

With a large terrace, it's a great spot to relax with a few pints or, better still, the carousel – an assortment of glasses or flutes that has helped make this brewery revered across the province.

Microbrasserie du Lac Saint-Jean
120 rue de la Plage, Saint-Gédéon; tel: 418 345 8758, https://microdulac.com.
One of the better stops for refreshment on the Lac Saint-Jean circuit, this lively microbrewery has a terrace and a small selection of stellar ales, such as a Belgian amber, all crafted with regional ingredients.

Microbrasserie La Memphré
12 rue Merry Sud, Magog; tel: 819-843 3405, https://lamemphre.com.
Kick back at this pleasant bar with views of Laker Memphremagog from the veranda. Enjoy tasty local beer and quality pub food, including juicy burgers, poutine and onion soup with red ale beer and melted cheese.

Microbrasserie Tadoussac
115 rue Coupe-de-L'Islet, Tadoussac; tel: 418-235 1170, www.microtadoussac.com
Tadoussac's very own brewpub knocks out some excellent craft beers, from the tasty IPA de la Traverse to the refreshing Ponton 5 pilsner, paired with a simple menu of pizzas, sandwiches, cheese and charcuterie.

Le P'tit Caribou
125 chemin Kandahar, Mont-Tremblant; tel:

819-681 4500, http://ptitcaribou.com.
At the height of the ski season, Mont-Tremblant buzzes with a lively après-ski scene, especially at popular Le P'tit Caribou, which is consistently voted one of Canada's best ski bars. Join the cocktail-fuelled crowd until the wee hours. There's also a wide range of live music throughout the year.

Pub Le Mitan
2471 chemin Royal, Sainte-Famille; tel: 418-829 0408, www.microorleans.com/pub-le-mitan.
An inviting microbrewery and just about an essential stop in summer, Pub Le Mitan has a terrace overlooking the St Lawrence from which you can enjoy a fine selection of home-brewed ales.

Pub L'Oncle Antoine
29 rue St-Pierre, Québec City; tel: 418-694 9176, www.facebook.com/oncleantoine
Dark and claustrophopia-inducing stone brewpub tucked inside a historic residence that somehow rarely feels overrun; the sidewalk seating is a great spot for people-watching. The staff are friendly and there's an excellent choice of Québécois ales on tap and a stellar Scotch selection, too.

Le Saint-Pub
2 rue Racine, Baie-Saint-Paul; tel: 418 -240 2332, www.saint-pub.com.
A terrific brewpub with a few ales on tap, such as the Dominus Vobiscum, that are wildly popular throughout Québec

as well as a selection of ales that are brewed seasonally or for shorter runs.

LIVE MUSIC VENUES

Montreal
Bistro à Jojo
1627 rue St-Denis; tel: 514-843 5015, www.bistroajojo.com
This longtime joint calls itself the "Blues Temple of Montréal" – and it's an apt title. Since 1975, this low-lit, unpretentious spot has been serving up nightly blues shows.

Casa del Popolo
4873 blvd St-Laurent; tel: 514-284 3804, https://casadelpopolo.com.
"The House of the People" is a sofa-strewn, low-key Plateau spot with high-calibre spoken-word evenings, folk, rock and other concerts and events. It also has lively DJ nights and by day serves vegetarian soups and salads – try the goats cheese and red peppers with nachos – making it a mingle-worthy spot any time.

Club Balattou
4372 blvd St-Laurent; tel: 514-845 5447, www.balattou.com.
This popular club heats up with live world music, from Africa to the Caribbean, most nights of the week.

Club Soda
1225 blvd St-Laurent; tel: 514-286 1010, https://clubsoda.ca.
Large live-music venue that attracts a the best acts and has reached almost leg

endary status in Montréal. The club also hosts Jazz Festival and Just for Laughs shows and events. Tickets from $15–20. Open nightly for shows, generally from 8pm until closing, though times vary.

Les Foufounes Électriques

87 rue Ste-Catherine est; tel: 514-844 5539, www.foufouneselectriques.com
A bizarre name ("The Electric Buttocks") for a wonderfully bizarre bar-club venue. Known as Foufs, it's the best place in Québec for alternative bands, attracting a crowd from ravers to punks. Huge outside terrace perfect for summer evenings, and pitchers of beer are cheap.

THEATRE

Montréal
Centaur Theatre

453 rue St-François-Xavier; tel: 514-288 3161, https://centaurtheatre.com.
Montréal's main English-language theatre showcases a wide range of theatre, from the classics to contemporary.

Place des Arts

260 de Maisonneuve Blvd West, Quartier des Spectacles; tel: 514-842 2112; https://placedesarts.com
A massive complex with a comprehensive year-round programme of dance, music and theatre. The Orchestre Symphonique de Montréal (www.osm.ca), Orchestre Métropolitain (https://orchestremetro-politain.com) and L'Opéra de Montréal (www.operademontreal.com) stage regular concerts here.

Théâtre Rialto

5723 av du Parc; tel: 514-770 7773, www.theatrerialto.ca;
This grand old theatre with a glorious Beaux Arts facade dates back to 1923–24, and is designated a National Historic Site of Canada. Revitalized in 2010, it now hosts varied programming throughout the year, from theatre to opera to concerts.

Théâtre St-Denis

1594 rue St-Denis W; tel: 514-849 4211, https://theatrestdenis.com.
This eclectic venue presents everything from blockbuster musicals to big-name concerts to comedy shows.

Québec City
Grand Théâtre de Québec

269 blvd René-Lévesque est; tel: 418-643 8131, https://grandtheatre.qc.ca.
The city's main theatre for the performing arts is the Grand Théâtre, which has a programme of drama, opera, dance shows and classical music.

Théâtre de la Bordée

315 rue St-Joseph est, Saint-Roch; tel: 418-694 9721, https://bordee.qc.ca.
Head to this long-running theatre for well-attended small-scale plays.

Théâtre Le Capitole

972 rue St-Jean; tel: 418-694 4444, www.lecapitole.com.
Just outside the city walls, Le Capitole hosts dinner theatre, cabaret and flashy musicals.

BOOKS AND FILM

Québec has gradually started to appear more frequently on TV and cinema screens in recent decades, but for such a beautiful part of the world representation remains surprisingly thin – at least in English. French language movies and TV shows have been knocked out in Québec for decades, but rarely get much attention beyond its border. Québec-made movies *Incendies* (2010), *Monsieur Lazhar* (2011) and *War Witch* (2012) were all nominated for Oscars. Most recently, Québec filmmaker Xavier Dolan's *It's Only the End of the World* picked up awards at the Cannes Film Festival (2016) and the Québec Cinema Awards (or Prix Iris; 2017).

Similarly, English-language publishers have tended to skip translations of the province's best French-language writers (of which there are many), which don't sell in large numbers. Mordecai Richler (1931–2001) was perhaps the most successful English-language writer to hale from Montréal. Though he's known for writing about the Jewish community in Canada, he also tackled Québec nationalism.

BOOKS

Fiction

The Apprenticeship of Duddy Kravitz by Mordecai Richler. French-Canadian, working-class and Jewish – Yiddishkeit was Richler's (1931–2001) bag. He was the laureate of the minority within a minority within a minority. All his novels explore this theme with broad humour and pathos. In The *Apprenticeship*, his best-known work, Richler uses his early experiences of Montréal's working-class Jewish ghetto in an acerbic and slick cross-cultural romance built around the ambivalent but tightly drawn figure of Kravitz.

Black Robe by Brian Moore. The story of a missionary's journey into New France in the 17th century – typical of Moore's preoccupations with Catholicism, repression and redemption.

The Body's Place by Élise Turcotte. Turcotte is one of several leading Francophone contemporary female writers in Québec; this powerful coming-of-age novel takes places over one summer in the life of teenage girl.

Hysteric by Nelly Arcan. Arcan was one of Québec's most exciting writers before tragically committing suicide in 2009. This harrowing novel examines of the way society objectifies and belittles women. See also her controversial *Whore*.

Poems & Songs by Leonard Cohen. A fine collection from one of Montréal's most famous sons, a 1960s survivor who enjoyed critical acclaim as a poet before emerging as a husky-throated crooner of bedsit ballads.

Surfacing by Margaret Atwood. Canada's most eminent novelist is not always

A variety of books on display

easy reading, but her analysis, particularly of women and society, is invariably witty and penetrating. The remote landscape of northern Québec plays an instrumental part in an extreme voyage of self-discovery.

Two Solitudes by Hugh MacLennan. Landmark novel that examines the seeming chasm between English and French cultures in Québec, set around the time of World War I.

Non-fiction

Celine Dion: My Story, My Dream. Québec's pride and joy was born into a working-class family in Charlemagne, just outside Montréal, in 1968. An honest and easy to read autobiography, first published in 2000.

Crucible of War: The Seven Years' War and the Fate of the British Empire in British North America, 1754–1766, by Fred Anderson. Lucid and extraordinarily well-researched account of this crucial period in the development of North America. At 800-odd pages, it's perhaps a little too detailed for many tastes, but it's a fascinating read.

Citizen of the World: The Life of Pierre Elliott Trudeau Volume One: 1919–1968 and **Just Watch Me: The Life of Pierre Elliott Trudeau: 1968–2000**, by John English. Two brilliantly written and researched volumes on Québec's best-known, most flamboyant (an uncommon characteristic in Canadian politicians) and definitely most divisive prime minister.

Made in Quebec: A Culinary Journey, by Julian Armstrong. In depth exploration into Quebecois cuisine, which remains relatively unknown outside the province. Written by a veteran food writer for *The Gazette of Montreal*.

A People's History of Quebec, by Jacques Lacoursière and Robin Philpot. Short and accessible history of the province, from the settlement of the St. Lawrence River Valley by the French through to the independence movement.

A Yankee in Canada by Henry David Thoreau. Though it can be hard to come by these days, Thoreau's description of the journey he took up the St Lawrence River from Montréal to Québec City in 1850 still makes compelling reading.

FILM AND TV

Black Robe, 1991. This historical drama – based on the Moore novel – follows the travails of Jesuit missionary Father LaForgue as he tries to convert the native Algonquin peoples of 17th-century New France. It was shot mostly in the Saguenay–Lac-Saint-Jean region.

Barkskins, 2020. Historical drama series based on Annie Proulx's book. David Thewlis stars as Claude Trepagny, the local seigneur in the early colony of New France. It was filmed in Québec.

Jesus of Montreal, 1989. This French Canadian comedy drama put contemporary Montréal on the map, as its follows a group of actors producing a passion play in the city (Saint Joseph's Oratory on Mount Royal).

ABOUT THIS BOOK

This *Explore Guide* has been produced by the editors of Insight Guides, whose books have set the standard for visual travel guides since 1970. With top-quality photography and authoritative recommendations, these guidebooks bring you the very best routes and itineraries in the world's most exciting destinations.

BEST ROUTES

The routes in the book provide something to suit all budgets, tastes and trip lengths. As well as covering the destination's many classic attractions, the itineraries track lesser-known sights. The routes embrace a range of interests, so whether you are an art fan, a gourmet, a history buff or have kids to entertain, you will find an option to suit.

We recommend reading the whole of a route before setting out. This should help you to familiarise yourself with it and enable you to plan where to stop for refreshments – options are shown in the 'Food and Drink' box at the end of each tour.

For our pick of the tours by theme, consult Recommended Routes for… (see pages 6–7).

INTRODUCTION

The routes are set in context by this introductory section, giving an overview of the destination to set the scene, plus background information on food and drink, shopping and more.

DIRECTORY

Also supporting the routes is a Directory chapter, with our pick of where to stay while you are there and select restaurant listings; these eateries complement the more low-key cafés and restaurants that feature within the routes and are intended to offer a wider choice for evening dining. Also included here are some nightlife listings and our recommendations for books and films about the destination.

ABOUT THE AUTHOR

Stephen Keeling worked as a financial journalist for seven years before writing his first travel guide and has since written numerous titles for Rough Guides. Stephen lives in New York City.

CONTACT THE EDITORS

We hope you find this Explore Guide useful, interesting and a pleasure to read. If you have any questions or feedback on the text, pictures or maps, please do let us know. If you have noticed any errors or outdated facts, or have suggestions for places to include on the routes, we would be delighted to hear from you. Please drop us an email at hello@insightguides.com. Thanks!

CREDITS

Explore Québec
Editor: Aimee White
Author: Stephen Keeling
Head of DTP and Pre-Press: Rebeka Davies
Head of Publishing: Sarah Clark
Picture editor: Piotr Kala
Cartography: Katie Bennett
Photo credits: Shutterstock 1, 4ML, 4MC, 4MR, 4MR, 4MC, 4ML, 4/5T, 6TL, 6MC, 6ML, 6BC, 6/7T, 7MR, 6/7M, 7MR, 8ML, 8MC, 8ML, 8MC, 8MR, 8MR, 8/9T, 10/11, 12, 12/13, 14, 15L, 14/15, 16, 16/17, 18/19, 20, 20/21, 22, 23L, 22/23, 24ML, 24MC, 24MR, 24ML, 24MC, 24MR, 24/25T, 26, 27L, 26/27, 28/29, 30, 30/31, 32/33, 34, 35L, 34/35, 36, 36/37, 38/39, 38/39, 40, 40/41, 42, 43L, 42/43, 44/45, 46, 47L, 46/47, 48, 48/49, 50, 51L, 50/51, 52/53, 54/55, 56, 56/57, 58, 59L, 58/59, 60, 60/61, 62/63, 64, 65L, 64/65, 66, 66/67, 68/69, 70, 71L, 70/71, 72, 72/73, 74, 75L, 74/75, 76/77, 78, 78/79, 80, 81L, 80/81, 82/83, 84, 84/85, 86/87, 88, 89L, 88/89, 90, 90/91, 92/93, 94, 95L, 94/95, 96, 96/97, 98/99, 100, 101L, 100/101, 102, 102/103, 104ML, 104MC, 104MR, 104MR, 104MC, 104ML, 104/105T, 106/107, 108/109, 110/111, 112/113, 114/115, 116/117, 118/119, 120/121, 122/123
Cover credits: Shutterstock

Printed in China

First Edition 2021

No part of this book may be reproduced, stored in a retrieval system or transmitted in any form or means electronic, mechanical, photocopying, recording or otherwise, without prior written permission from Apa Publications.

Every effort has been made to provide accurate information in this publication, but changes are inevitable. The publisher cannot be responsible for any resulting loss, inconvenience or injury.

DISTRIBUTION

UK, Ireland and Europe
Apa Publications (UK) Ltd
sales@insightguides.com
United States and Canada
Ingram Publisher Services
ips@ingramcontent.com
Australia and New Zealand
Booktopia
retailer@booktopia.com.au
Worldwide
Apa Publications (UK) Ltd
sales@insightguides.com

SPECIAL SALES, CONTENT LICENSING AND COPUBLISHING

Insight Guides can be purchased in bulk quantities at discounted prices. We can create special editions, personalised jackets and corporate imprints tailored to your needs.
sales@insightguides.com
www.insightguides.biz

INDEX

MAP LEGEND

● Start of tour	–––· Province boundary	Ferris Wheel
→ Tour & route direction	⊖ Border crossing	⊙ Metro station - Montréal
···· Extra tour	Ⓜ Museum	Funicular
❶ Recommended sight	✚ Church	▲ Summit
❷ Recommended restaurant/café	圕 Library	Park
★ Place of interest	👺 Theatre	Important building
❶ Visitor centre	✉ Post office	Urban area
✈✦ Airport / Airfield	✚ Hospital	Transport hub
		National park